VALUES

What They Are &
How We Know Them

VALUES

What They Are &
How We Know Them

JOHN T.
GOLDTHWAIT

 Prometheus Books

59 John Glenn Drive
Amherst, NewYork 14228-2197

Published 1996 by Prometheus Books

00 99 98 97 96   5 4 3 2 1

Library of Congress Cataloging-in-Publication Data

Goldthwait, John T.
    Values : what they are & how we know them / John T. Goldthwait.
        p.   cm.
    Includes bibliographical references and index.
    ISBN 1–57392–007–X (pbk. : alk. paper)
    1. Values. I. Title.
BD232.G616   1996
121'.8—dc20   95–43778
                                                         CIP

Printed in the United States of America on acid-free paper

For Chris

Contents

Preface

"Values! These days, everything is values!"

This is the distressed cry of a reader trying to make sense out of the political, economic, and social news, not to mention the advertising, in the public media.

Family values. American values. Or both together—American family values. One columnist said the defining issue in the Clinton-Bush election was family values.

"What's wrong with our schools is that they don't teach our youngsters any values!" That is the message of many an editorial and letter to the editor that I have recently read in my daily papers.

One Florida school board got into trouble recently by deciding that the teachers were to teach their children that America has better values than any other country. Much to their surprise, the teachers went on strike over the issue! The school board, they claimed, was infringing on their *right of free speech,* a long-standing *American value.*

The teachers had probably been touched by the trend toward multiculturalism, which encourages schools to make their students familiar with one or more other cultures besides the American, without being judgmental about the value of those cultures. The students, if anybody, would be the ones to form value judgments about whether the values of one culture were better than those of another.

An insurance company, American Family Insurance, capitalizes on its name and on the "family values" fad to offer a new series of life insurance policies called "American Family Values" policies. It states in its direct-mail advertising that it is offering these policies to those who believe in families and America's future, and who obey the law!

The Heritage Foundation solicits members and money with a statement the recipient is supposed to sign, saying, "I share your belief in individual liberty, limited government, the free market, and the importance of Western civilization. I want to help the Heritage Foundation defend these values."

President Bill Clinton, in his January 26, 1994, State of the Union message to Congress and the American people, urged that we strengthen "the basic values of work and responsibility."

But what *are* values? What are we talking about when we talk about values? When we talk about value judgments, what is it that we are judging? How many of us can state clearly and authentically what a value is?

We tend to answer with examples such as the following: "Oh, you know, patriotism, fairness, democracy, religion, that sort of thing; God, mother, and country." But examples are not definitions. What we tend to see as issues in the multiculturalism question is what we call "cultural values." Yet it seems as if we ought to be able to define what a value *is* before we go looking for the values in a foreign culture.

Most of us have some acquaintance with value judgments but

probably could not give a definition of what a value judgment *is*. Most of us probably agree with the widespread idea that all value judgments are "matters of opinion," but do not know why. Most of us are able to identify *some* value judgments as such, when we encounter them, but we are uncertain whether we recognize all of them or just exactly what makes them value judgments. Most of us are unaware of many of the value judgments that occur in our experience. And most of us—probably all of us!—have felt the frustration of trying but failing to break down someone else's stubborn and seemingly unreasonable belief in a value judgment.

The question "What is value?" is one of the oldest in the province of philosophy. It was phrased by Plato, in the fourth century B.C.E., as "What is the good?" About all the progress made so far toward finding an answer has been, beginning in the eighteenth century, to substitute the word *value* for the word *good,* perhaps to make it a little clearer that the sought-after item was thought to be a property, along with size and shape and color, of the things that were good, that had value.

In 1952 Everett W. Hall published a careful analysis, in his book *What Is Value?*[1] which showed that value is not a property of anything. Neither is it a relation between things, such as between the valuable diamond ring and its owner. Hall had to confess, however, that even though he was in the position of knowing what value is *not,* he still did not know what it *is*.

I believe, however, that I have found the answer. In this book I offer my solution to the nonphilosopher, the person who doesn't have a technical background in this subject. The more philosophically inclined reader may look at my *Value, Language, and Life,*[2] where I have systematically developed and argued for the position sketched in the present work.

Both specialists and the layperson realize that even though they make value judgments and accept or reject the value judgments of others, they would like to know a bit more about what they are talking about when they do this. This book, then, is a plain-language, user-friendly treatment of a very important question.

This study is intended to help you:

1. understand "values";

2. understand "value judgments" and identify them when you encounter them in speech or print;

3. tell the difference between value judgments and statements of fact;

4. identify value judgments that you already accept;

5. generate new value judgments and formulate your own value judgments in clear language;

6. decide whether to accept or reject value judgments that others urge upon you;

7. find support for value judgments that you want to persuade others to believe;

8. examine and carefully criticize value judgments and the support for them that others offer to you, and decide whether to accept, reject, or suspend judgment on them;

9. understand what you read when it contains open or hidden value judgments;

10. understand the relation between values and moral principles, and between values and art;

11. understand the role of values in your culture;

12. compare the values embraced by your culture with those embraced by other cultures;

13. understand the relation between values and individual choices;

14. understand "special-case" uses of the word *value,* which sometimes have nothing to do with value;

15. understand why you have a right to your own value judgments.

This book will proceed step by step, largely by means of examples, each chapter introducing just one main idea. As you take each step forward, you will be able to accomplish more and more of the goals in the above list, thus filling out your knowledge of value judgments. It will help you to control them fully in your thinking, your problem solving, and your discussions. This means that you will be able not merely to talk competently about value judgments, but to form them, use them, and convince others that they should accept value judgments from you.

I hope, moreover, that you will find, as I have, that studying and getting acquainted with values is a fascinating and highly pleasurable pursuit.

NOTES

1. Everett W. Hall, *What Is Value?* (New York: Humanities Press, 1952).
2. John T. Goldthwait, *Value, Language, and Life* (Amherst, N.Y.: Prometheus Books, 1985).

1

What Is a Value Judgment?

Let me begin by offering some samples of what we mean by "value judgments":

List One

Life is good!

This is good coffee.

Spot is a good hunting dog.

The School for Scandal is a good eighteenth-century play.

Playing backgammon is a good way to spend an otherwise dull evening.

All of these value judgments contain the word *good*, and seem to be saying about the subject introduced that it is *worth something*, it *has value*. These all are *favorable* value judgments.

Here is another list of sample value judgments with a different kind of effect.

List Two

Last year was a bad year.

Yesterday's weather was pretty bad.

Two thousand dollars plus his trade-in for an eight-year-old car was a bad deal.

It ran twenty-one weeks on Broadway, but essentially it was a bad play.

Playing endless games of solitaire is a bad use of one's time.

The value judgments in this second list, all using the word *bad,* are saying that something is of poor quality, that it isn't what you would want if you had a choice.

Value judgments of this sort, denying that something has worth or value, or saying that it has only low worth or value, are called *negative* or *adverse* value judgments.

Now let us list some more examples. In our third list we will have value judgments that are *positive* or *affirmative,* like those of the first list, but they will not use the word *good* to make that point. In fact, they will all use different words to get that meaning across. And in our fourth list we will offer *adverse* value judgments, again no two using the same word to convey their message.

List Three

This year's Panther is a great deal better than last year's model.

In sending his younger brother to college, Culbertson certainly did the right thing.

That glue was the best that I could get during those wartime conditions.

The workmen did a superior job of laying Mr. Blackburn's concrete floor slab.

When Betty entered and walked toward me down the aisle, she looked absolutely beautiful.

When we can talk her into keeping the minutes of our society's meetings, she does it really well.

The sample value judgments in the third list show that there are other words besides *good* to express positive value judgments. In fact, we will eventually see that there is a virtually infinite range of them. To be able to recognize these no matter what form they occur in is a skill well worth learning.

List Four

When my garden became overrun with watermelon vines, it looked worse than ever.

Building his new fence so that half of it was on his neighbor's property was the wrong thing to do.

Having his stamp collection thrown into the muddy stream was the worst thing that could have happened to Wilmer Blaine.

At the beginning of every meeting, the creed of the lodge was always said, and it was always said poorly.

Now you are being beastly to me.

We can see that the same can be said about adverse value judgments, namely that there is a great variety of ways in which they may be expressed. We shall shortly see the key to recognizing these adverse judgments as well. Thus we can be aware of the expression of any and all value judgments that others put before us—and for that matter, we can eventually recognize which of *our own* ideas are not factual statements but value judgments.

In the next chapter we will lay the background for value judgments. Then we will begin a full survey of their characteristics, so as to arrive at a definitive concept of just what they are.

2

Statements of Fact, Judgments of Value

The examples of value judgments given in the first chapter should suggest that value judgments are very common, that we very frequently hear or read them, and that in fact we very frequently speak or write them.

Those value judgments are cast in the form of sentences. But not all sentences express value judgments. Let us look at other uses that we have for sentences.

Some sentences, having a different form from those just described, are created in order to ask questions. Others express commands. These two kinds are easily distinguished from statements by their form, the former by the question mark or questioning intonation of the voice, the latter by the omission of a subject to indicate that the intended subject is "you," the hearer or reader of the command. But there are also certain sentences that, unlike questions or commands, have the *appearance* of statements but do not function in the same way. Some of these kinds of sentence include the following:

Ceremonial statements, such as "I'm fine, thanks." Even people with splitting headaches will say this, to return a ritual greeting rather than report truthfully on their own health.

Statements used as questions: "The taxi has arrived?"

Statements that mainly do a job: "I christen thee U.S.S. *Saratoga*!"

Expressions of immediate feeling: "Well, I swear!"

Various meaningless or nearly meaningless expressions: "Well, I'm a son of a gun."

Those are the exceptions. Most of the complete sentences that we hear that are not value judgments are *statements of fact,* and in situation after situation they far outnumber the value judgments.

Here are some sample statements of fact:

Abraham Lincoln lived for fifty-six years.

Wells drinks two cups of coffee with breakfast every morning.

Gibson's dog is a Weimaraner.

Sheridan's play *The School for Scandal* was first performed in 1777.

David Hume used to play backgammon.

Any hurricane that hits these shores will be accompanied by a flood of ocean water.

These statements are implicitly saying, "Here is some information. This is the way it is (or was, or will be). This is something that actually happened (or does happen, or will happen)." These statements do *not* suggest what is good or bad about the subject matter, or what it should be like, or what is wrong with it. They appear simply to be making a report of the actual facts. The above sample statements of fact are very typical of much of the essay, historical, journalistic, and textbook writing that we regularly encounter. Statements of fact like these provide the backdrop for most of the value judgments we encounter.

In everyday talk and in the printed word, statements of this factual kind appear to outnumber the value judgments by a ratio of two to one or even higher—in some contexts by fifty or a hundred to one. I think you will agree, either immediately or after testing the idea in your experience, that there are many more of this sort of statement than there are of value judgments. Sometimes an entire essay or book chapter will contain nothing but statements of fact, with no value judgments at all.

In fact, the predominance of this declarative or descriptive kind of statement over the other tends to conceal the fact that there are two different kinds of statement, which tends to mislead us into applying the same rules and general principles to the value judgments that we do to the statements of fact. But *that is a dangerous way to proceed.* If we do not carefully distinguish between the two, we make the mistake of expecting results from value judgments that they simply cannot give us. This is another factor that makes the study of value judgments very much worth our while. When we learn to distinguish between these two chief types of statement, we put ourselves in a position to learn the limitations of each as well as how to take advantage of each kind's respective strengths.

It may help to clarify the difference between the two kinds of statement if we set down in parallel columns some statements that are typical of each kind.

Statement of Fact	Value Judgment
This is a book on investing.	This is a good book on investing.
My father lived to be ninety-six years old.	My father lived ninety-six wonderful years.
She is one of Offenthal's sisters.	She is the most beautiful of Offenthal's sisters.

Statement of Fact	**Value Judgment**
Smoking pot is the thing we do.	Smoking pot is the wrong thing for us to do.
The author fully explains his idea in 135 pages.	The author fully explains his idea in 135 fascinating, superbly written pages.

Do you see the difference? The factual statements are giving information, stating what is the case, or what has happened or is happening or will happen. The valuative statements, on the other hand, assert a degree of goodness of the subject being discussed. They ascribe worth or value. In them, a *judgment* on the facts is expressed.

It is time now to note an important point. With the statements of fact above, *the main point of the statement* is to offer a fact. In contrast, the main point of the value judgment is to *tell whether, and in what degree, the person or thing mentioned has value.* This difference is expressed in the English language by the wording or the emphasis within the sentence. In typical cases, simply adding an appropriate adjective will do the trick.

But we should also note that value judgments are statements that actually *do* impart information ("explains his idea in 135 . . . pages"); but this is secondary. The sentence's main task is to affirm *whether and to what extent the thing mentioned has value* (in everyday language, "whether it's any good, and if so, how good it is"). In one of the above examples, the description "fascinating, superbly written" expresses that the thing mentioned (the book of 135 pages) does have value—and, in a subjective way, tells how much value the book has.

This chapter has taken the first step toward analyzing any discussion you may read or hear. That step is to boil down the discussion preferably to one or a few statements, or (nearly the same thing) to pick out from the discussion the most important statement(s) it contains, and then to *identify whether the statement is a statement of fact or a value judgment.*

In order to do this, the first essential is to determine the *main thing the statement is saying.* In the more prosaic discussions that our occupations and other activities present to us, this is not usually difficult. In the case of some works of literature, philosophy, or politics, it might actually be difficult and worth debate or consulting an expert commentary. But even using such aids, you probably prefer to study the matter and make up your own mind, finding evidence for your decision in the statement itself and its surrounding context. This book will help you in this quest. The next few chapters will assist you in deciding whether a given statement is one of fact or a judgment of value.

3

Recognizing Two Different Kinds
of Statement

"Tell it like it is, man!"

This mandate was popular during the reform movements of the 1960s and 1970s. It was used to call up facts as opposed to lies. Now, without worrying too much about the lies, we will begin to work our way to a fuller understanding of the statements of fact. We recognize that statements of fact and value judgments are both specific kinds of statements, but that the difference between them is important. So far, we have made a rough distinction, saying that the value judgments express ideas of worth, while statements of fact express only information about a situation: what has happened, what is now happening, or what will happen.

Everything we have said so far about the distinctive content of these statements is true, but we need to be more exact and precise. Here we will show how we can be more precise about the statements of fact, and why we should be. Let's begin by saying that the topic of "fact and value" is a philosophical briar patch. Some philosophers are at home in it, like clever rabbits, but others have had a pretty scratchy experience and avoid it, like Brer Fox. The philosophers have various definitions of both *fact* and *value,* and they take sides and argue for or against their respective definitions.

We do not need to get involved in these thorny questions in order to accomplish the objectives of this book. We simply side-step them by confining ourselves largely to the study of *statements.* Thus what we will deal with now is not the facts and values themselves, but the things people say about them, the statements by which people express what they think the facts and the values are. It is a major purpose of our undertaking to understand these statements; to prepare us to manage them as they come into our lives; and, later on if we choose, to strive for a better, fuller understanding of the facts and values themselves. This book then becomes a tool of understanding to help you reach your own comprehension of the problem that keeps the philosophers busy. Later on, we can venture to suggest a view about what roles facts and values play in our lives.

As a first step toward precision, we will use the word *proposition* to refer to those statements, whether statements of fact or value judgments, that we are studying. It is the tendency in our English-speaking culture to use the word *proposition* to mean a statement that is being taken more seriously than usual. For example, we usually term the sentences in a referendum for voters or in a geometric proof *propositions,* not *sentences* or *statements.* Using this term will help us sort out statements in the background from those in the forefront of our attention.

In the remainder of this chapter I shall show how we can profitably apply the term *proposition* to our understanding of what we have been calling statements of fact. Then in chapter 4 I'll do the same thing for those that we've called value judgments.

Normally, a person making a statement of fact is concerned to "tell it like it is," to relay from his mind to yours exactly the factual content of a situation: what has happened or what is the case.

When people use the word *fact,* they associate the idea of truth with it; therefore, the phrase *statement of fact* seems to many to imply a statement that is true. Instead, we'll use the phrase *fact-claiming proposition* because we need to talk about the statements *as* statements, regardless of whether they are true or false—and sometimes we will not know whether they actually are true or false.

We are aware that sometimes people attempt to assert, affirm, or proclaim facts but end up not doing it. Perhaps they don't know what the facts actually are; or they know them but don't express them accurately; or else they know them but choose to lie or hide the facts from us. We need a term that will fit the kind of sentence we're speaking about even when it is not true, a deliberate lie, or an inaccurate statement. This is something we can do with the phrase *fact-claiming proposition* that we could not do with *statement of fact.* In other words, a fact-claiming proposition is a statement of the kind that is normally used with the intention of conveying a truth, but in some instances falling short of it. Such a proposition looks as though it is trying to pass on a fact to us, even though, for several possible reasons, it may fail.

Let's look at a few examples.

1. There is milk in the refrigerator.

2. My subscription to the daily newspaper costs eighty-four dollars a year.

3. The mayor is elected by a vote of the city commissioners, who elect one of themselves to that office.

4. Sherlock Holmes had an ability to discover a great deal of information in ordinary things like muddy footprints and military buttons, things that served him as clues in solving crimes.

5. New York City is a little bit south of the Panama Canal.

6. The author expects to make several million dollars on sales of the present book.

7. This guy was, you know, one of the people who have that job, y'know, that job of going around making sure that people aren't, well, the way he's watching out for.

8. Your congressman represents you by casting his vote in the House as he believes the greatest number of his constituents want him to vote.

9. The economic recession we are facing in the next two to five years will be just like the Great Depression of 1929–1939.

10. I think that the economic recession we are facing in the next two to five years will be just like the Great Depression of 1929–1939.

11. The year 2000 is the first year of the twenty-first century.

12. Columbus discovered America—well, at any rate, an island in the West Indies—in 1492.

If you were asked whether these are value judgments, you would not have a hard time saying no. You would recognize instantly that the statements do not appraise anything by telling how good or how bad it is. Rather, each of the above propositions has the look of those statements that purport to "tell it like it is," that is, relate the state of affairs, or what actually happened.

Now I suggest that it is the form, the shape, of these statements, the way they are constructed and the way that they function or appear to function in their contexts, that gives the clue that they belong to the fact-affirming statements; along with that there is the absence of anything in their chief thought that indicates value.

Let's see how each of our sample fact-claiming propositions succeeds in its attempt to state the truth.

1. The first example, relative to its writer (myself), is true. As I write, there actually is milk in my refrigerator.

2. The second statement is also true with respect to me, the author. However, if someone else in another city had made it, the statement might well be false. The truth or falsity of sentences often depends on the situation in which they are presented.

3. The third statement is true of some cities but false of others. (What? Can a statement be both true and false?)

4. Sherlock Holmes is a fictional character. If you are going to call the statement about him true, you'd better qualify your decision by saying something like "with respect to the detective stories by Sir Arthur Conan Doyle." A schoolboy who reads Sherlock Holmes stories has no trouble calling this statement true, though adults know it has only a fictional "truth." The schoolboy accepts the surroundings in the Holmes stories as a reality, and does not concern himself much with the difference between those surroundings and our "real world." We who have more experience, however, keep that fictional world well separated from the "real world."

5. There is no such way to rescue the statement about New York—it's simply false!

6. As regards this book, this is of course a false statement. The author is kidding you. Many an apparent statement of fact, especially in conversation, can accurately be called a tease.

7. The poor fellow who originated this remark may have known something, but he doesn't know how to express it. We can tell that he is trying to assert a fact but not succeeding. Even though we don't know what he's driving at, we can classify his sentence as fact-claiming.

8. The statement about your congressman is intended by some speakers, such as teachers of social studies, as true. But others who make it might intend to be ironic—seeming to tell the truth but implying its opposite.

9. This statement is a prediction of the future—but nobody has ever been to the future. Although there is more or less likelihood of the statement's accuracy based on current information, we simply cannot yet know with absolute certainty what the future will actually bring economically. The statement is indeterminate as to truth or falsity. Still, it is fact-*claiming,* because it is of the kind that attempts to state what *will* be rather than what *ought to* be.

10. If the speaker of the previous item were to make this statement also, we could take it as true. That is because the main thought has changed. The *main* thought is about "what I think," not about what the economy will be like. Moreover, people rarely try to deceive us about what they think, and there is little reason in such a matter as this why they should deceive us. Whether the sentence is true or false depends on whether its speaker really does think what he says he thinks, *not* on what the economy will actually be like.

11. This sentence is the subject of some disagreement. Evidently certain people understand a century to consist of every year whose designation starts with a given multiple of 100. Against these are the people who define a century as a series of a hundred years. Those who say that the year 2000 starts the twenty-first century will do so at the cost of having to allot to the first century only nine-nine years, contrary to either definition of a century.

12. So far as we can trust historical records, this statement is true. It's also an example of someone trying to speak with more than usual exactness. "An island in the West Indies" expresses much more precisely what Columbus actually found than the vague "America."

This list of fact-claiming propositions should show us several things. One is that the sentences work for us in the way we expect them to work, so long as we regard them as efforts to tell the truth.

Yet, as my comments on the examples given show, it is surprising how many such sentences are not out-and-out, black-or-white, no-two-ways-about-it clear cases of true assertions. In our ordinary discussions, this fact is usually so little likely to be troublesome that we are not even aware of it. My reason for introducing these sample fact-claiming propositions was explained in terms of our expecting them to tell the truth. We have habits of taking sentences within their contexts and making interpretations that enable us to understand the intention of their speaker or writer, and thereby to understand how, and how much, they actually convey truth.

Similar habits evidently inform us also which sentences assert values rather than facts. The most likely source of problems is our tendency not to recognize that value judgments work differently from factual statements, and hence to expect them to function in exactly the same way as fact-claiming propositions. Therefore, we expect at least some of them to justifiably be called "true." In the next chapter we will have to improve on this false understanding, as we show how to be more precise about value judgments.

4

How Claiming Relates to Truth

Let us introduce a phrase to increase the precision of our thinking about value judgments, just as we did with the phrase *fact-claiming propositions* for the factual statements.

Our official phrase from now on for a sentence stating a value judgment is *value-claiming proposition*. We use the word *proposition* for the same reason as stated in chapter 3 and *value-claiming* for a reason very similar to that for *fact-claiming*. Many philosophers have attempted to tell us what value is, or (what amounts to the same thing) what "the good" is. Yet while philosophers surely have some sort of theme in common, they do not widely agree on any definition of *value*. We do know, however, that people are very widely agreed upon what a *value judgment* is; that is, a value judgment is an expression used to assert a value— to relate a particular thing that should be considered to be a value. Thus it is apparently easier for us to recognize a passage that *talks about* a value than it is to recognize and identify the value itself.

Let's look at a sampling of *value-claiming propositions,* which is much more inclusive than the sample lists given in chapter 1.

Value-Claiming Propositions

1. Honey is good. (This is a filling-in of the formula "*X* is good," often used by philosophers as the standard form of a value judgment.)

2. Honey is better than sour milk.

3. Aside from milk, honey is the best natural food for children.

4. It was right for Harry to leave a generous tip for the waitress whom he had asked for so many services.

5. The new painting over Mother's mantel is simply beautiful.

6. Although the Cézanne has more interesting color combinations, the Renoir painting is the more beautiful of the two.

7. The most beautiful thing in God's whole creation is the body of a human female.

8. You have done an excellent job.

9. Curly is the wisest man I have ever met.

10. Of all his sons, the eldest, his pride and joy, amounted to the most in adult life.

11. Charity is a virtue.

12. It is good to be generous toward one's defeated enemies.

Some Negative or Adverse Value-Claiming Propositions

1. Catching a cold is bad.

2. Catching a cold is worse than getting a cold sore.

3. Catching a cold on her wedding day is the worst fate that can overtake a bride-to-be.

4. Even though her daughter hadn't written to her for years, it was wrong for the mother to cut the girl entirely out of her will.

5. What had before been a fine, prosperous farm was now, after the passing of the hurricane, an ugly, broken shambles.

6. Bad conduct is much more ugly than a bad appearance.

7. Burgleville, where Schmidt grew up, is the ugliest town in all of Pennsylvania.

8. Your performance on that math test was not exactly wonderful.

9. Montague's manners left something to be desired.

10. Of all his sons, the eldest, his pride and joy, amounted to the least in adult life.

11. It was unfair to give the entire inheritance to William and leave Albert out of the will.

12. To park every day in the space reserved for the handicapped, when he had neither a handicap himself nor a permit for the handicapped, was wrong.

Some Less Obvious Value-Claiming Propositions

1. That dangerous machine is not worth what Dad paid for it.

2. You ought to be ashamed of yourself!

3. Kugel does a very professional job of sliding into home plate.

4. Don's work on his customers' cars was always of the highest quality.

5. Von May is one fireman who deserves a gold medal.

6. In spite of the buildup we had heard, Tom's performance on the oboe was not very outstanding after all.

7. Hudson's passing and running could not have been improved upon.

8. In the argument between his mother and his mother-in-law, Clarkson should not have taken sides.

9. In his mode of address to his firm's customers, Steuben was unfailingly courteous and considerate.

10. While Dingle's characters were well drawn, his plots always left something to be desired.

Now we come to the crux of the matter. It is time to state and explain the essential, defining characteristics of fact-claiming and value-claiming propositions.

Fact-claiming propositions are statements that express states of affairs or events. They state something objective, which would ordinarily be described or narrated in the same way by any competent observer.

Since the possible coverage of fact-claiming propositions is extremely broad, we have been using expressions to try to fill in and make more familiar what we mean by "states of affairs" and "events." What we mean by *states of affairs* is "the way things are," "the way things were," "the way things are going to be," "how it really is (or was or will be)," "how it actually was," and equivalent phrases. Since states of affairs have a present, a past, and a future, I use these phrases as reminders of how great a coverage is packed into that brief expression *state of affairs.*

Similarly, for *events,* some phrases appropriate for expanding on this term are "what happens"; "what did happen"; "what will happen"; "what's going on"; "what was going on"; "what will be going on"; "what so-and-so is doing (or was, or will be doing)"; "what took place (or is taking place, or will take place)"; and other expressions in the various tenses that express those ideas.

This summary is intended to fill out the notion of what the word *fact* covers, and therefore of what sort of thing the fact-

claiming propositions can express. They tell *how things are,* or *how things happen.*

Value-claiming propositions, on the other hand, express how states of affairs or events *ought* to be.

Most of us know without any need for explanation what, in general, the word *ought* means. Therefore, let's first dwell on other aspects of value-claiming propositions, and then later concern ourselves with the niceties and nuances of the term *ought.*

Following are lists of the ways in which the value-claiming propositions relate to the idea of *ought.* We will see that *every value-claiming proposition has the idea of* ought *at its very foundation.*

Easy Translations

1. "These are good paint brushes" means "These paint brushes are as paint brushes ought to be."

2. "This is a good strawberry" means "This strawberry is just as strawberries ought to be."[1]

3. "Joe Leventhal is a better tennis player than Bobby Schale" means "Joe Leventhal is more like what a tennis player ought to be than Bobby Schale is."

4. "Joe Leventhal is better with his backhand than Bobby Schale" means "Joe Leventhal uses his backhand more in the way that it ought to be used than Bobby Schale does."

5. "Joe Leventhal's victory leap is the best in the whole tennis world" means "Joe Leventhal's victory leap is the most like what a victory leap ought to be, more than that of anyone else in the whole tennis world."

And Some Negatives . . .

1. "These are bad paint brushes" means "These paint brushes are not as paint brushes ought to be."

2. "My brother's paint brushes are worse than these" means "My brother's paint brushes are less like what paint brushes ought to be than these are."

3. "These paint brushes are the worst in the world" means "These paint brushes are the least like what paint brushes ought to be, of all the paint brushes in the world."

4. "Tom Terrell sings poorly" means "Tom Terrell does not sing as a singer ought to sing."

5. "George Gable sings worse than Tom Terrell" means "George Gable sings even less as a singer ought to sing than Tom Terrell does."

6. "Gabriel Grafton is the worst singer of all" means "Of all singers, Gabriel Grafton sings the least as a singer ought to sing."

Let's get some exercise on the contrast between *is* and *ought* with another list of examples.

Examples of the Contrast between Fact-Claiming and Value-Claiming Propositions*

1. Some Reuben sandwiches are just Reuben sandwiches. This is a *good* Reuben sandwich.

2. I sold my Apple Computer stock when it was at 47½, but I ought to have held onto it until it went up to 65.

3. The highway could easily have been made completely straight. However, it was better to have a variety of gentle curves, so that drivers would not become sleepy or hypnotized by the monotony of a straight road.

---

*The first part of each example is fact-claiming; the second part is value-claiming.

4. We awoke to the strident tones of a loud siren nearby. This was a good thing, for it warned us of incoming enemy aircraft.

5. Murchison always sang "Yankee Doodle" in the key of C. He ought to have sung it in the key of E flat.

6. Kenneth took the money from his mother's purse and left home at the age of fourteen. He ought to have stayed with her and earned money to help her bring up the younger children.

7. Whenever Grace went out she usually wore shades of pink and red. Her complexion being what it is, she ought to have worn yellows and blues instead.

These examples should underscore the difference between the way things *are,* or *were,* or *actually did happen,* and the way that things *ought to be,* or *ought to have been,* or *ought to happen.* Observe that *the way things are* and *the way things ought to be* are not necessarily the same.

Some other examples will further illustrate:

1. Their showroom was only ten by fourteen feet, and was lighted by a single overhead fixture. It ought to have been twice as large and much better lighted.

2. I went to bed at half past midnight last night. I ought to do better than that—I ought to get to bed at least by eleven if not by ten.

3. Although the speed limit was fifty-five miles per hour, she was going seventy-five. She ought to have had greater concern for her own and other people's safety.

Notice the kind of difference there is between the fact-claiming and the value-claiming parts of each of these examples. In the first, the showroom was said to be ten by fourteen feet, and that statement could be proved by measuring the showroom. It was also said to be illuminated by a single ceiling fixture, and that, too, could be proved by looking at and counting the fixtures. But the claims that it ought to have been at least twice as large and better lighted are matters of opinion, which cannot be subject to the test of measurement. Who is to say that "twice as large" is the right degree of improvement, not one and a half times or three times as large? Who is to define "better lighted"? The actual showroom is out there in the world, and can be measured and its features counted. But the ideal showroom that the critic is speaking about doesn't actually exist. Therefore, you can't go and measure it or count its ceiling fixtures. You might *agree* with the value judgment made by the person who is speaking critically of the showroom, but neither you nor this critic can *prove*, objectively, what has been said about how large and how well lighted the showroom *ought to be.*

With regard to the second example, it can be verified (by one's memory, say, or by asking members of one's family) whether the speaker did in fact go to bed at half past twelve. But there is nothing to inspect, nothing to measure, no separate world of *ought* into which to fit the "ought to" of "I ought to get to bed by eleven. . . ." And even if a doctor has told me that I ought to get to bed by eleven, the doctor has nothing to inspect or measure, the way we measure a roll of yard goods to make sure it really is thirty-six inches or more wide. His value-claiming statement is strengthened by his status as a doctor, but it still concerns a world that is not the actual world. It belongs to a conceptual world to which all the value claims pertain. That's the kind of statement the value-claiming propositions are, even when there is acknowledged authority and expertise behind them.

As for the third example, it is possible to verify objectively both the assertion that the speed limit was fifty-five and that "she" was driving at seventy-five. The first is verified by driving the highway concerned and looking at its speed limit signs. The second may be verified by asking the driver herself what her speed was, or by consulting witnesses such as drivers whose cars she passed, or by asking the arresting officer who ticketed her. But the value judgment, "she ought to have had greater concern for her own and others' safety," does not have its subject matter in any realm that we can go to, to inspect it. Be sure to grasp this point: *Though vast numbers of persons agree on a value judgment, that does not prove it to be true.* It just shows that many, many persons believe it. For vast numbers of persons to believe such a value judgment as "life is precious" does not prove it to be true any more than the belief of vast numbers of persons that the world is flat proves that the world is indeed flat. Just as numbers of believers do not prove factual claims, neither do they prove value claims.

How, then, does claiming relate to truth? When one utters a fact-claiming proposition, one speaks with the appearance of someone who is attempting to tell it like it is, to set a truth before the hearer. But telling alone, making the claim alone, is not enough to guarantee that the proposition is true. When one utters a value-claiming proposition, one may seem to be attempting to tell it like it is, but one is actually referring instead to how things ought to be. In the next few chapters, we will study value-claiming propositions more closely, to work toward an understanding of how they can be justified.

NOTE

1. R. M. Hare, *The Language of Morals* (New York: Oxford University Press, 1964), p. 110.

5

When We've Got It Good

When have we "got it good"? When everything is as it ought to be! When we've got it good, we make affirmative value judgments, and "it" (whatever "it" is) gives us no cause to make adverse ones.

The way things *ought to be* and the way they *are* are *not necessarily* the same, but, fortunately for us, in some cases they are the same! This is so when we justifiably use a positive or affirmative value-claiming proposition. And it's when we can do *that*, that "we've got it good."

We have already seen some affirmative value-claiming propositions in chapter 4. Let's look at a few more.

1. Martha is a good cook. (This means, "As a cook, Martha is as she ought to be," or "Martha cooks as a cook ought to cook." If we're among those whom Martha cooks for, we've got it good!)

2. The Panther is a good car. (That is, "The Panther is as a car ought to be," or "The Panther has the characteristics that a car ought to have.")

3. The Panther exceeds its competition. ("The Panther is more like what a car ought to be than competitive cars are.")

4. "Butler Motors is North Chicago's leading Panther dealer!" ("Butler Motors is the most like what a North Chicago Panther dealer ought to be." Granted that there's probably only one Panther [or Ford, or Chevrolet, or Dodge] dealer in North Chicago, not much has been said. Still, whoever said it probably believes that Butler Motors is as an auto dealer ought to be—that the factual and the ideal coincide.)

5. *April in the Park* is the best film I've ever seen. (*"April in the Park* is the most like what a film ought to be of any film I've ever seen.")

6. It's a good thing that we've got Thaman for quarterback. ("The fact that we've got Thaman for quarterback is as it ought to be," or "Having Thaman for quarterback is as it ought to be.")

7. Investing in bonds for income is better for me now than investing in stocks for growth of capital. ("Investing in bonds for income is more like what investing ought to be, for me, than investing in stocks for growth of capital.")

8. Herman Woodrow is the best flugelhorn player in the field of amusement today. ("Herman Woodrow is the most like what a flugelhorn player ought to be of all flugelhorn players in the field of amusement today.")

9. This wine is excellent. ("This wine is the most like what a wine ought to be of any wines that could properly be compared with it." The word *excellent* not only means "espe-

cially good" but connotes comparison, i.e., that this wine is "better than others.")

10. These peaches are unsurpassably sweet and tasty. ("These peaches are so sweet and tasty that no other peaches could be more like what peaches ought to be.")

You will notice that in the above examples the underlying pattern of "translation," of finding an equivalent statement to the value-claiming proposition, is this:

"X is good" means "X is as it ought to be."

It is true that in the above "translations," often there are many more ways of expressing value judgments than simply saying "is as it ought to be." That is because in the expression of value judgments there are often many more words than "is good": we qualify our thoughts, making them more precise, and as exact and communicative as our situation seems to require, and enrich them with related details. Even in the very simple example, "Martha is a good cook," it won't do just to say "Martha is as she ought to be," because the original assertion about Martha's merits was narrowed down to cooking. That's why we need the additional wording.

When the value judgment is a little farther away from the language of the standard formula, as in our third example, we have to ask ourselves exactly what the value-claiming proposition is saying, and make sure that we get just that, nothing more and nothing less, into our "translation." The "translation" given above for this example contains both the idea of *exceeds,* which expresses the idea of winning out over competition, and the idea of "better than" when the cars are compared feature by feature. As you read the full list of "translations," which is to say, equivalent statements given after the value assertions in the above examples, you can see how the equivalent statement in each case expresses "ought to be," and expresses it with respect to just what was said within the limits established by the wording of the first version.

To confirm that "*X* is good" means "*X* is as it ought to be," reflect on your own experience. Isn't it true that whenever you say something is good, you are implying, at least in general, that it is as it ought to be? Surely you aren't saying that it *isn't* as it ought to be, or even that it is merely indifferent compared to how it ought to be. When you have classified something as good, most likely you are satisfied with it, accepting it as it is and not intending to change it. You don't change it because you consider it to be as it ought to be. On the other hand, when you set out to change something, you are demonstrating a judgment that it is *not* as it ought to be, and to that extent is not good.

The chief point of this chapter is that when we make affirmative value-claiming propositions, we are affirming that something *is* as it ought to be. Correspondingly, when we make negative or adverse value-claiming propositions, we are affirming that something *is not* as it ought to be.

Therefore, we are now in a position to define *value*: *A value is a conception of how something ought to be.*

Accordingly, a *value-claiming proposition* is a proposition asserting how something ought to be.

Our next chapter will identify some signs that help us pick out value-claiming propositions in contexts in which they occur.

6

Useful Signs

Now we are ready for some signs and clues of value-claiming statements. Interpreting them correctly depends upon knowing that value-claiming propositions are about the way things ought to be, and that fact-claiming propositions are about the way things are.

The best sign of a value judgment, obviously, is the word *ought*. Suppose you saw these sentences:

1. Daniel ought to quit smoking.

2. The Walconian rebels ought to surrender.

3. Charles ought not to play jazz.

4. Even though Wilbur's eyesight is 20/20 and his reflexes are quick, he ought not to drive so fast.

You know at once that these are value-claiming statements. Here's why. First you would have noticed the word *ought* in each sentence. That strongly suggests classifying the statements as value-claiming. But in order to be sure, you would have checked your impression by asking, "Does the sentence state something that ought (or ought not) to be?" Thus the most probable *sign* of a value-claiming statement is the presence of the word *ought*. But while the *sign* usually points us in the right direction, the actual *test* of a value-claiming statement is always the *question,* "Is it about the way things ought to be?"

Signs, however, are rarely infallible. Consider these next examples:

5. Since his plane left Los Angeles sixteen hours ago, he ought to be in Hong Kong by now.

6. What's the product of 23 times 895.99? Oh, that ought to be somewhere between 20,600 and 20,625.

In spite of the presence of the word *ought,* these are *fact-claiming* statements. If you had been given the propositions "George ought to go to Hong Kong," and "If George is going to be in the diamond business, he ought to be in Hong Kong," you would know that these are value-claiming, telling how things ought to be with respect to George's obligation (ought to go to Hong Kong) or welfare (ought to be in Hong Kong). But our fifth example is not about anyone's obligation or welfare. It is a way of stating that it takes less than sixteen hours to fly from Los Angeles to Hong Kong, and of reflecting that if we reason using a knowledge of George's hour of departure and of the estimated flying time, we may soundly conclude that by now his trip is over. *Ought, in this special kind of case,* means "we are entitled to believe."

The sixth example, concerning the product of two figures, makes this point more strongly. The numbers are higher than most of us are accustomed to working with in our heads, but the speaker (perhaps better at mental arithmetic than most of us) is reasoning with the quantities involved. He is saying that we are entitled to believe that the product is between 20,600 and 20,625. And he is shown to be correct, because when we do the multiplication on our handheld calculator, we find that it is actually 20607.77. This is a factual matter, susceptible to clear and indubitable proof; therefore, it is not a value claim but a factual assertion.

Additional signs of value-claiming propositions, signs that are often good, though not infallible, clues, are the words *good, better, best, bad, worse,* and *worst.*

Consider the following examples:

7. That was a good movie.

8. Heard's safety gloves are better than Motroni's.

9. This is the best waffle iron that money can buy.

10. The closing of the local bank places a bad strain on our domestic economy.

11. Fruehberg's stabbing by his drunken son was a worse end than Haines had ever foreseen for him.

12. Flooding in the Midwest this year was the worst in American history.

True to principle, these may be translated into ought-language, as follows:

7a. That movie was as movies ought to be.

8a. Heard's safety gloves are more like what safety gloves ought to be than Motroni's are.

9a. This waffle iron is the most nearly like what waffle irons ought to be of any waffle irons that money can buy.

10a. The closing of the local bank places a strain on our domestic economy that is not as it ought to be.

11a. The end Fruehberg came to by his drunken son's stabbing him was less as it ought to be than any end Haines could have foreseen for him.

12a. Flooding in the Midwest this year was the least what it ought to be than of any year in American history.

These translations show that in each example, the presence of the key word (*good, better, best, bad, worse, worst*) was a sign that the sentence was a value judgment, a value-claiming statement. All the sentences were about what ought, or ought not, to be. These key words are thus signs that can usually be depended on.

However, issues concerning language are rarely simple. In this matter, we have to recognize that there are some exceptional uses of the terms *good, value,* and related words that don't conform to the translation "as it ought to be," and that require special explanation. Words like these, though they often appear in the main thought of a value-claiming proposition, may yet in some contexts convey a nonvaluational meaning. When a term has several meanings rather than only one, it is the context that determines one's choice in interpreting a sentence. We must keep this in mind when we are looking for the most accurate "translation" of sentences whose words are most often found in value-claiming propositions. Let us look at some of these special cases.

First case. In certain contexts, the word *good* may have special associations instead of or along with the general meaning, *as it ought to be.* Sometimes that special meaning is more important than the general meaning of approval. An example is, "A hammer is good for driving nails." A variation on this sentence, with added emphasis, is, "What a hammer is good for is driving nails." Either sentence is rather precise about the way in which the hammer is spoken about, i.e., with respect to the act of driving nails—not cutting wood, not fixing flat tires, not baking cakes, not even pulling nails out of wood even though most hammers are so made that they can do that as well as drive them. Whenever either of these two sentences about hammers is used, the main thought is, "A hammer *is used for* driving nails." Our phrase *is good for* has come to mean "is used for." However, the sentences still convey approval, at a *lower,* secondary level of importance, so that a more complete filling out might be, "A hammer is used for driving nails (and does a good job of it—drives nails the way they ought to be driven)."

Second case. Again, "This light bulb isn't good any more" means pretty explicitly "This light bulb is burned out." It doesn't even mean "This light bulb doesn't fit the size of socket that is in the new lamp"; our usage has stripped away other possible meanings of *good* with respect to light bulbs. It makes their goodness confined solely to the function of giving light. Yet even with that restriction, we still sense an undercurrent of meaning of "as it ought to be," for in our widespread judgment, light bulbs ought to be capable of giving light, and if they are not, then they are not good. "This light bulb isn't good any more" means not only "This light bulb is burned out," but also, on a secondary level, "This light bulb no longer is as it ought to be."

Third case. A student reads an algebra problem that instructs him to "Fill in the value of *x* with a whole number." In this special context there is present no notion of value or of the good in the more general sense, no way of getting "Fill in the as-it-ought-to-be of *x* with a whole number." The word *value* is simply used in a different way than usual, in the fields of mathematics and some of the sciences, to mean simply the temporarily assigned meaning of a variable term. As you can see, it is necessary to keep within that context to make any sense out of "Fill in the value of *x* with a whole number."

Fourth case. Another example in which the context narrows down *good* to a specific meaning is, "This offer is good only until November 30." Try your hand at stating in words exactly what *good* means in that expression. (After trying, you can find some versions, with discussion, on pp. 135–36.)

Other cases. There are other specialized uses of the word *value* in such fields as music (the duration of a note), painting (the specific quality of an area on the scale of light to dark), and mining geology (the presence in an ore of something worth extracting). So far as *good* is concerned, there are probably as many special meanings of the word as there are fields in which it can be applied. Perhaps that is why value theorists see it as the archetype of value-asserting words.

You can no doubt find still other special cases. I suspect that for any that you may find, the idea of *as it ought to be* will still be present on a secondary level even though it is not the main meaning of the statement.

As you have been able to see, it is the main thought of any statement that determines whether it is a fact-claiming or a value-claiming proposition. It is not a meaning on the level of a modifier of a modifier of a modifier. Take "This is a piano." It's a simple statement, probably serving to introduce the word by which a certain musical instrument is known, or else pointing out the object that is known by that word, a word with which the listener has already become acquainted. The gist is that the sentence tells what the object *is*. But let's add a single word: "This is a good piano." What we have now, because that's the way the English language works, is a value-claiming proposition. The main thought has become not what this *is* but what its quality is—in other words, whether, being what it *is,* it is as it ought to be; i.e., whether as a piano it has the characteristics that a piano ought to have.

In determining whether any sentence is fact-claiming or value-claiming, it is necessary to identify the main thought of that sentence. Fortunately, most of us are quite capable of doing that from long practice in using the language. And even if two of us disagree on what the main thought is, and consequently disagree about whether the sentence is fact- or value-claiming, we at least have located the source of our disagreement, and that itself is an important advantage in conducting our discussion. It is always better to know where we stand.

Now let's consider the word *bad*. Like *good,* it has special meanings that arise in particular cases. It is probably true that with *bad* the context more readily indicates what the special meaning is. It may also be true that with this word in its special cases there is a stronger flavor of valuation than what is usual in the cases of *good.* We continue with our list of examples:

13. I'm sorry I can't help you lift those bales. I have a bad back.

14. I can't start my car. It has a bad battery.

15. You don't dare make a pie out of those apples, because they have gone bad.

And now to explain these examples of "bad":

In the thirteenth example a "bad back" is a pretty specific condition of health. A person with a "bad back" cannot readily lift things or exert much strength, because he will feel pain in doing so, too much pain to tolerate. Moreover, this condition is often the result of some injury, and to perform any but the lightest tasks is likely to make the injury itself worse. Of course, the tone of the sentence conveys the meaning, "This is not as it ought to be," but the specific features of the injured back are conveyed more dominantly as a main meaning of the sentence. That this is a special case is shown by the fact that not everything that is "bad" is a condition of being unable to lift heavy objects. Thus the sentence conveys certain information about the speaker's physique, and secondarily indicates that this is not as it ought to be.

In our fourteenth example a "bad battery" very specifically is a battery that does not develop enough power to supply the necessary current to enable the starter of a car to turn the crankshaft. Such a battery of course is not as it ought to be. However, mechanics and auto buffs understand the phrase "bad battery" to mean exactly this, not a leaking battery or one that is the wrong size for the car involved. Thus these specifics are the main concern of this example, and the idea that the battery is not as it ought to be is of secondary importance.

As for our fifteenth example: Very simply, apples that have "gone bad" are apples that have begun to rot. *Bad* in such a sentence as this has that very specific meaning. Once again, it is quite clear that the apples are unacceptable, but on a secondary level; the reason the apples are unacceptable is stated in the information given on the first level, namely, that they are rotten.

What emerges from this discussion is the importance of keeping aware of what is the main idea, and what is a secondary idea, in any statement that is worth our attention. We classify these statements as fact-claiming or value-claiming according to their main idea. And when a word normally used as a sign of a value judgment is used instead to convey factual information, we classify its statement as *fact-claiming* on the whole, while in some cases we note that it is value-claiming on a secondary level. The main thrust of it is to convey facts (what a hammer is used for, whether a light bulb will still give light, whether lifting a weight will cause pain, whether a certain battery fails to start a car, or whether certain apples are rotting). Thus the signs had best be treated as indications of the *possibility* that the statement is value-claiming. They are not such certain indicators that no further thinking about whether or not a statement is value-claiming is needed.

7

How Do We Know What Ought to Be?
A First Look

It is very likely that by this time you have raised the question "How do we know what ought to be?"

While this question does not have a simple answer, we can at least move toward a partial answer. Then we can use our future experience to build on it for ourselves so that as we go from one situation to another, one value judgment to another, we may become ever better at supplying to ourselves our answer, our conceptions of what ought to be. That means that value judgments can be made about value judgments, that there are better and worse value judgments and that for the most part we can decide which are which.

The question "How do we know what ought to be?" is natural, in fact inevitable. Any curious and inquiring mind will be attracted to it and will urge that it be answered. In moving toward that goal, let us first examine the question itself by breaking it down into its constituent parts: an "ought" and knowledge of what that "ought" is.

"How do we know . . ." These words show that we *assume* that we are going to *know,* not guess, not merely suppose, what ought to be. It is human and natural to assume this rather than the opposite—that we will not know, or cannot know, what ought to be, even while we go right on making value judgments on all of life's matters from the most trivial to the most complex.

". . . what ought to be?" These words show that we *assume* that there is a situation that ought to be, and that it is within our grasp to understand it, perhaps to bring it about.

The typical inquiring mind now, I suggest, expects that once we get the answer to the question "How do we know what ought to be?" we will put our stamp of approval on those value-claiming propositions that match up with "what ought to be," because now we "know" "what ought to be," and this will give us a clear track to bringing about the changes indicated. Very soon, then (we think), we'll have a world consisting wholly of what ought to be and—what then? We will have arrived in Paradise, I suppose.

But I regret to suggest that reality isn't that easy on us. What I believe has happened in this little scenario is that our language has led us astray. I suggest that the reason we ask how we know what ought to be is that in many situations we are looking for a different kind of an answer, an answer like that to a factual question, which might be formulated in the words, "How do we know the way it is?" This question is appropriate when we are working out the next stages in the solution to certain kinds of problems, as we indicate in such expressions as "When we know how the market is, we will know how to invest our money"; and "When we find out what the cause of Alzheimer's disease is, we will know what kind of drug to formulate in order to arrest it"; and "As we learn more about the distribution of stress in the structural framework of a bridge, we will become better able to prevent the breakdown of bridges when they are in use."

The question *"How do we know* the way it is?" shows that we are aware that we need a method of inquiry. In the first instance, we need a method that shows us the nature of the investment market; in the second, a method that discloses the causes of Alzheimer's disease; and in the third, a method for investigating the stress patterns of structural components of bridges. These things, we feel sure, will supply us with facts about the problem situations involved and enable us to arrive at their solutions. Consequently, when dealing with problems involving value, it is only natural that we ask the question "How do we know (not the way it is, but) the way it ought to be?"

Here I am going to take the first step in developing our answer to this general question, but I am going to save subsequent steps for later stages of our project. We are, as it were, ascending to our goal on a spiral staircase, and to get to the top we have to pass around from one side of the staircase to the other as we ascend, then to the first side again, then the other, and so on until we are at our goal. And if all that existed were the part of the staircase that was on only one side of the stairwell, we could never get around to all the stages we need to pass through, and we'd never reach our objective, the top position from which we could look down and see it all.

The first step, then, any time we are working our way through some immediate problem, is to find a value judgment that will help us solve it. And we have to do this for practically any problem we might face. Whenever we have a problem, we need a value judgment, a statement of what ought to be done; we need it because it is the value judgments, the value-claiming propositions, that guide us and tell us what to do. The following examples will illustrate.

Problem: I've unintentionally hurt my wife's feelings.
Value Judgment: I ought to show her that I really want to make her happy.
Outcome: Since flowers usually make her happy, I send her a bouquet of red and yellow roses.

Problem: My son is not interested in anything having to with school, but only in what concerns his bicycle.

Value Judgment: I ought to get him to transfer his attention from his bicycle to the things he should be learning in school.

Outcome: I devise study units to show how a bicycle could come into the subject matter, and I get him interested in everything from tire pressures, the spelling of name brands, and the physics of pedaling to stories about great cyclists, bicycle tours of Europe and the U.S.A., and even accident insurance.

Problem: My lawn mower won't start.

Value Judgment: I should make sure that fuel is getting to the engine.

Outcome: Since there are several possible reasons for fuel not reaching the engine, I make sure that there is fuel in the tank, that the cutoff valve between the tank and the carburetor is open, that the throttle is open, and that there is no blockage in the rubber tube between the tank and the carburetor.

Here we have seen how a part of solving a problem of the everyday sort is seizing upon a value judgment that tells us something to do. Then we do it, and either that solves the problem or else it puts us farther along on the way toward solving the problem by eliminating a measure that did not work.

Thus the first step in answering the question "How do we know what ought to be?" is, "by having sufficient specific knowledge about the field in which a problem has arisen, and thus by being able to supply value claims based on what is usual in that field." Regarding my wife, I know that it is more normal for her to be happy than to nurse hurt feelings, so I generate a value judgment that should help restore that normal situation. Regarding my son, who loves his bike more than school, I know that normally a child likes learning when there is a motivation for it, so I find a value judgment that brings together the motivation with the material that I believe he should learn. In the field of lawn mowers, I regard the ability to start as normal. Therefore, I generate a value judgment that will establish, or restore, the normal situation, which will follow from seeing to it that the mower engine has an adequate supply of gasoline.

Don't let it be forgotten that these problem-solving value judgments are of the underlying pattern, "Here's what you ought to do." They serve as specific rules of conduct for the particular problems we are trying to solve. And they assume that we have a sufficient knowledge of the field or fields in which our problems are likely to arise. Of course, that assumption may be faulty, but it points out for us the necessity of mastering a number of fields of knowledge, so as to become more and more proficient in finding the needed value assertions and to show an increasing wisdom, as we go through our lives, in knowing what ought to be.

This first look at answers to the question "How do we know what ought to be?" is very limited, but at least it's a start. It is most useful for day-to-day situations, not the world's great problems. But it shows the basic pattern—the assertion "Here's what you ought to do"—that will underlie moral and other kinds of problems calling for value judgments to reach solutions.

We will attack this important question again in later chapters, until we arrive at an answer that covers all the necessary ground.

8

Some Ways We *Don't* Know
What Ought to Be

It will help to fill in the total concept of *ought* if we separate it from some of the things that it is *not*. We'll keep "what ought to be" separate from certain ideas that we perhaps associate with it but that emphatically are not the same thing. These include "what I like," "what I wish," "what I desire," and "what I want."

Perhaps you have allowed the thought to cross your mind, "Oh well, a value is anything you like." It may sometimes seem that simply liking anything is enough to make it a value, that liking it is enough to constitute it as the way things ought to be. But *ought* is not the same thing as *like*. Some people *like* to use cocaine, but that is not the same as saying that they *ought* to use it. We have all heard friends say something like, "I love chocolate ice cream, but I ought never to eat it." This difference is extremely obvious. However, it is worth repeating so that we will remember it when someone hears the suggestion that values are what we judge ought to be, and responds by saying, "Well, then, you mean that values are simply whatever you like." One of the points of this book is that values are *not* whatever you like.

Consider the following examples.

Affirmative Statements

1. I like chocolate. (Does this mean the same thing as "I ought to eat plenty of chocolate"?)

2. I like to lie in bed in the morning instead of getting up and going to work. (Does this mean "I ought to lie in bed in the morning instead of getting up and going to work"? Doesn't it more strongly suggest "I ought to get up and go to work even though I like lying in bed"?)

3. I like the quick high that I get when I shoot heroin. (Does this mean the same thing as "I ought to shoot heroin when I want a quick high"?)

Negative Statements

4. I don't like paying taxes. (Does this mean the same thing as "I ought not to pay any taxes," or "I ought not to have to pay any taxes"?)

5. I don't like driving on the left side of the road when I'm in England. (Does this mean the same thing as "I ought not to drive on the left side of the road when I am in England"? Or "I ought not to have to drive on the left side of the road when I am in England"?)

6. I don't like taking the medicine that my doctor prescribed.

7. I don't like visiting my boring uncle in the nursing home.

Are the items of the above two lists fact-claiming or value-claiming? That is, do they assert the way things are (or are not), or instead do they assert the way things ought to be (or ought not to be)?

The examples in both lists are *fact-claiming*. That is because each of the examples given is a statement of what *actually* is the case, of what someone *actually does* like or dislike. It is a definite event in one's life when he or she takes a liking (or an aversion) to something. It is a happening, a fact. A statement expressing it, then, is a *fact-claiming* statement which can be proved by asking the person concerned about his or her likes. It is a statement about *the way things are,* not about *the way things ought to be.*

This shows that a value is *not* whatever you *like.* Therefore, a sentence of the pattern "I like *X*" does *not* mean the same thing as "*X* is good" or "*X* is as it ought to be." By similar reasoning, we can show that a value is not what you *want,* or what you *desire,* or what you *are interested in,* or what you *wish for.* But let us continue our treatment of what one *likes* and its relation to value.

It is far from true that anything that somebody likes is the way that the world ought to be with respect to that particular thing. Here are comments on the examples from the above two lists.

On 1: Liking chocolate does not confer value upon it, and doesn't mean the same thing as that it is valuable. I can like procrastinating, being lazy, freeloading, and exaggerating, but that is no sign that these practices are as they ought to be and that, therefore, I ought to procrastinate, be lazy, and so on.

On 2: This speaker probably believes that as an employed person he *ought* to get up in the morning and go to work. He has said he likes to stay in bed *instead of* going to work. If he did not believe that he ought to go to work, he would have been unlikely to say "instead of," and would just as likely have mentioned some other option rather than going to work—shopping, tennis, mowing the lawn. There is a strong probability that, in this instance, what the person *is* doing and what he/she *ought* to do don't coincide at all, but are pretty much opposed to each other.

On 3: A fair majority of the population of nearly every modern society believes that a person *ought not* to shoot heroin (that is, take
heroin in a vein through a hypodermic syringe), for nearly every
law-making society has passed laws against this practice. So
within the framework of those societies, we can say with confi-
dence that a person *ought not* to shoot heroin. This speaker—let's
call him Tom—is probably aware that what he likes is unlawful.
But he says he likes the result. Do we therefore conclude that Tom
ought to shoot heroin? Obviously we don't, or we'd change those
laws. *Liking an action or activity is not reason enough to assert
that it ought to be done.*

    Do we say that Tom *ought not* to like the high he gets? No,
there isn't any way we can get "Tom ought not to like it" from
"Tom likes it." Neither is there any way we can get "Tom ought
not to like it" from "Tom ought not to do it." We can assert that although Tom likes to *do* it, he *ought not* to do it, because it is
against the law. Moreover, this is one law that is enacted for the
good of the health and welfare of the individual as well as of the
society, and that is another reason Tom ought not to do what the
law forbids him from doing. For Tom to shoot heroin gets bad results for Tom. Of course, those who simply do not believe in law
will not agree.

On 4: Who is so naive as to believe that not *liking* to pay taxes re-
lieves one of the obligation—the *ought*—to pay them?

On 5: The safety both of the general public, whether on wheels or
on foot, and of the driver himself are at stake here. The person
complaining *ought* to drive as other drivers do, because of the
laws and of the habits and expectations of other drivers. To drive
otherwise invites disaster.

On 6: If I have gone to a doctor for treatment, and he has prescribed a medicine for me, I am implicitly recognizing already that
I ought to take his prescription. So I *ought* to take it. I don't *have*
to like it.

On 7: Perhaps here the obligation, the *ought*, is the weakest of any of the examples. However, the point is still seen that what I *like* and what I *ought to do* are quite different.

The strongest proof of the difference between liking and the *ought*, I believe, is the circumstance that we know in our own minds, the times when we have acted on the value claim "I ought not to do that" in spite of our liking to do it. And, conversely, we act on the value claim "I ought to do that" in spite of not liking to do it. If *liking X* were what it takes to make *X* a value, we could never have this experience. In this way we easily show that what a person *likes* and what *ought to be* or what one *ought to do* are quite different things. Therefore, in our reasoning, we may not substitute one for the other.

Another conclusion to be drawn is that people can go against their own likings when they know it's for their own good. Few of us like having a tooth pulled, but we accept having it done and go through with it when we are convinced it is necessary. Surely all of us have had the experience of doing something of this kind, and it helps us to accept the necessity of doing so when we can articulate to ourselves the distinction between *like* and *ought*.

Finally, we can see that every once in a while in public discourse someone speaks confusedly about likes and dislikes as values. "Susan Smith despises abortion" may be perfectly true, but that is not enough by itself to make true the statement that "Being against abortion is one of Susan Smith's values." Instead of abortion, take amputation. Susan Smith may well despise amputation, but she would probably agree with informed medical opinion that in certain cases, such as extreme gangrene, amputation ought to be performed. Hence Smith's dislike is not the same as her belief about whether amputation ought ever to be performed. Thus while "Susan Smith despises abortion," a *fact-claiming* proposition, may be true, and "Abortion ought never to be performed," a value-claiming proposition, may also be one of Susan Smith's beliefs, the first statement does not automatically imply the second. No doubt Susan Smith, who despises abortion, also believes that abortion ought never to be voluntarily performed, but she must realize that her own, or anyone's, dislike of it is not enough by itself to support a general public view that abortion should never be performed. Perhaps she is willing to marshal other, less emotional, reasons.

Let's conclude with two further examples:

8. "But I freely admit that there are many features of the Utopian Republic which I should like—though I hardly expect—to see adopted in Europe." These words of Sir Thomas More, from the conclusion to his *Utopia,*[1] are *not* literally a value-claiming proposition. Rather, they are a factual report by the narrator that he likes something, namely certain features of Utopia. But we can *infer* that the author also believes in a value claim that he has not explicitly stated, namely, "Many of the features of the Utopian Republic ought to be adopted in Europe." When there is a value judgment very clearly underlying the words of an author or speaker, we may say that the value claim is *implicit* in the text that he has actually given us. Implicit value claims will be discussed further in chapter 17.

9. I like eating all these delicious sweets, even though they are making me fat.

One fact stated in this example is, "I like eating . . . sweets," and another is, "they are making me fat." Both can be tested and proved or disproved. But most people think of the word "fat" in this context as having an additional meaning of "too heavy, weighing too much." Therefore, the example implicitly *suggests* the value judgment, "I ought not to eat these sweets," even though that is not directly stated. And far from being equated with "I like . . . ," it is the opposite of it. Thus *fat* conveys a negative value. Many words do this in their contexts, and some normally do it without regard to the context. These are *value-attributing words,* described in chapter 18.

Now that we have seen that liking something in and of itself is not enough to make it a value, we are able to handle several other expressions that people sometimes seem to regard as equivalent to *ought.* Some of them *want, desire, wish, hope,* and *approve.* These have the same relation to *ought* that *like* has with *ought.* Superficially they seem to constitute X as a value, because when one likes or wants or desires X and then attains it, there is satisfaction, and we believe that satisfaction is good. That is, we believe that satisfaction is something that is as it ought to be, thus when satisfaction can be brought into our experience it ought to be done. Many of us, maybe nearly all of us, will agree that satisfaction itself is a value, something that ought to be. But that is why this confusion arises—our minds jump from the thing wanted to the satisfaction we believe will result. When Joe Colson wants to marry Mary Parham and gets turned down, his best pal tells him, "Don't worry. You'll find some nice girl to marry, and you'll be just as happy." The pal, you see, is suggesting that Joe will have the satisfaction of happy wedded life even if it's not with Mary but with someone else. And he sees that any girl who is amorously inclined toward Joe will contribute to the satisfaction of married life with him—it doesn't have to be Mary.

Let us survey some more examples:

1. Bill wants to forget about his college loan instead of paying it back.

Bill very naturally wants to keep control of whatever cash he may receive, but he knows that both by terms of his contract and by common fairness he *ought* to pay back his college loan. What he wants and what he ought to do are clearly very different, because forgetting about the loan, which Bill wants to do, means that its repayment (the fair thing) will not happen; but not forgetting about the loan, which he does not want, means that its repayment will happen.

2. That old house is what I want.

This is a fact claim. Let us suppose it is a true one—I really do want the house. That does not in itself mean "I ought to have that old house," or "that house ought to be mine." It does not mean that the owner has to give it to me. Nor does it mean that the house is as it ought to be. There's a fellow who is wanted in four states. That's because he is *not* as he ought to be.

3. It is Millhouse's desire to control the political machine of Klackas County.

Many a politician desires to control a political machine, "and that's a fact"; but in the interest of the public there would be no individual who controls the political machine of his county. In fact, there would be no "political machine" in his county, because these by definition are organizations devoted to subversion of normal democratic processes rather than abiding by them. Thus if by this principle *what ought to be* were to be brought about, the politician's desire would never be fulfilled, and the public consensus would be that that desire was far different from what ought to be, rather than being the same thing.

4. This beach property on our idyllic tropical island surely is desirable.

The words *desire* and *desirable* are near-perfect synonyms of *want* and *wanted*. For the reasons given above, they are different in their meanings from *ought* or *as it ought to be*. There have been some attempts in the philosophy of value to understand the valuable as being the same thing as the desirable. This, however, is not my position, and is not consistent with my principal view, namely, that "that which is valuable" means "that which is as it ought to be."

5. When Sally was an adolescent girl, she wished that a handsome knight would come along on a white horse, sweep her up in his arms, and carry her off.

Sally had a beautiful fantasy, but *what ought to be* surely is nothing so unrealistic in this day and age. Now that Sally is older, she'll hopefully recognize that her adolescent wish should be left behind and that she should settle for a fairly good-looking fellow with a steady job and a second-hand Chevrolet.

6. We hope we'll win the Georgia lottery this week!

Naturally, everyone who has a lottery ticket hopes to be a winner. But how could *one* ticket holder justify the proposition that the winning ticket *ought* to be his or her ticket, rather than that of any of the other million or so ticket holders? In fact, it looks as though the odds are a million to one against that being the way things ought to be. In the culture of the gambling public, there is no person who has a greater claim than another to be the one who ought to become a winner.

7. I approve of a ten o'clock curfew for people under eighteen.

Those considerations that rule out "like" as the fountain and source of value also rule out "approve." There is a difference only in the nature of the meaning of *like* and *approve* as attitudes. We probably think of the extending of approval as being on a more reasoned basis than extending our likes or dislikes. Certainly it is possible to like something (such as sleeping late) that we do not approve of, or to approve of something (such as the necessary pain of a surgical operation) that we do not like.

But the point also must be made that X's being approved is not the same thing as X's being as X ought to be. Many a dubious driver earns the approval of being licensed by the driving examiners when his driving has not yet been perfected, has not become what it ought to be.

People under eighteen, in a crime-ridden city, could approve a curfew that keeps them and their peers off the streets in the evenings, while not really liking it. What ought to be, they will probably tell us, is a city in which there are no dangers traceable to people under eighteen or threatening to people under eighteen. So, until that condition comes about, they approve the curfew.

The important thing about this chapter on distinctions and differences is not the sample words that have been shown to be different in meaning from *ought* or *as it ought to be*. These are merely examples; there are others like them. What is important to learn is to gain the habit of examining every statement in serious discourse, to answer the question "What is this indicating—how it *is,* or how it *ought to be*?" When you know which of the two is the effect of the statement, you will know how to handle it and what you are doing if you decide to believe it.

The separation of liking, wanting, desiring, and so on from what ought to be does not simply dismiss them. *Sometimes* what one likes, wants, desires, wishes for, or hopes for is *also* what ought to be. It is realistic to recognize that the fact that I like X (where X is an activity or action) is sometimes a reason for deciding—along with other reasons—that I ought to do X. If there are not reasons to the contrary, the liking of X and the satisfaction to be gained from X *may* (and then again, may not) be what is needed to make me believe that I ought to do X. Similarly, the fact that I want X (where X is an object) is among the reasons I may consider for taking action to get X. And the same for desiring or wishing for or hoping for X. But the fact that X is often what I ought *not* to do, or have, is enough to show that no one of these is enough by itself to constitute X as a value.

NOTE

1. Thomas More, *Utopia,* trans. Paul Turner (Middlesex, Harmondsworth, England: Penguin Books, 1965).

9

How Do We Know What Ought to Be?
A Second Look

In chapter 8, you read that for a given thing, *X,* "I like *X*" *does not mean the same thing as* "*X* ought to be." Nor is it reason enough to justify *stating* "*X* ought to be." This was important, to keep our meanings clear, hence to keep our thinking clear. It was important to prevent the false impression from arising that "Value is anything you like," or that "If there is something you like, then that is therefore something that ought to be."

Our next point is that *some* of the things you like *are* things that ought to be, and *some* of them are things that ought *not* to be. Just as some cows are black and some are not, some things that ought to be are things you like and some are not. Being black doesn't make something a cow, and being liked doesn't make something a thing that ought to be. There is no necessary correspondence between one and the other.

In this chapter, we'll look at several (but by no means all) of the widely accepted ways we have of knowing what ought to be.

In general, we believe that a thing *ought to be* (or an action ought to be done), other things being equal, when (1) it contributes to: (1) human survival; (2) human health; (3) human knowledge; (4) human wisdom; (5) the order, tranquility, and progress of human communities and societies; (6) human mastery of the global and spatial environment; and (7) the spiritual well-being of the human soul.

The following list provides examples of value claims and justifications for them through reference to one or more of the principles stated above:

1. Whenever you ride in a car, you ought to fasten your safety belt. If the car were in a bad accident, wearing the belt could save your life.

2. Everyone should have some exercise every day, even if it is only a brisk walk for ten minutes. This keeps a healthy body tone and helps maintain one's strength.

3. Even though Hy is the owner of the business, he ought to take a little time off for a vacation now and then. It would be good for him to enjoy life outside of a business setting every once in a while.

4. Taxpayers ought to support the federal space exploration program. It is making immense contributions to science.

5. All Americans ought to read Benjamin Franklin's *Poor Richard's Almanac.* Even though it was written more than two centuries ago, they will be the wiser for it.

6. Adolescents should have training and practice in conducting meetings and passing legislation, because it will give them an understanding of how our government works.

7. Each community should install and continually expand a program to collect materials for recycling. Every bottle or can recycled is one less item that could pollute our environment.

8. When I was in college the dean urged that every student should spend at least fifteen minutes a week in meditation. He said it would help us understand the world around us and the orientation of our own souls within it.

Notice that nearly all of the justifications (the statement following the value assertion in each item) are fact-claiming. The only exception is, "They will be the wiser for it," which calls for a value claim about each reader of Poor Richard, since *wise* is a valuative term. It is very natural that most of the justifications should be factual, since it is of the nature of value beliefs to affect our situations in the world of fact.

By introducing these principles and showing how certain value judgments relate to them, we have taken a second step in the process of examining how we know the way things ought to be. In this step we have acknowledged certain highly important value-claiming beliefs that are abroad in our culture. You may agree with all of them, or perhaps you reject one or more. They are important to you nevertheless, because they round out your understanding of value judgments urged upon you by other people.

Now that we've drawn up a positive list, let's look at some negatives. A thing ought *not* to be when it: (8) threatens human survival; (9) damages human health; (10) inflicts pain; (11) suppresses human knowledge; (12) suppresses and/or inhibits human wisdom; (13) detracts from the tranquility and progress of human communities and societies; (14) interferes with or lessens human mastery of the global and spatial environment; and (15) inhibits or injures the spiritual well-being of the human soul.

I'll now set down for each principle a value claim that lends itself to justification by that principle, but I'll let you fill in for yourself the explicit justification from items 8 to 15.

9. Shirley ought never to do what she does—sit in the filled bathtub drying her hair with the electric hair dryer!

10. One ought not to smoke, and ought not to work in places with a smoke-filled atmosphere.

11. That hundred-decibel music from the joint next door should be done away with.

12. The teacher ought not to have been going through the copies of the weekly newsmagazine blacking out certain phrases with a marker, to make the copies safe for her children.

13. The revolutionary government of this banana republic ought not to have been calling for blind obedience from its citizens.

14. There should be no private armies in any nation—armies maintained by wealthy individuals or interest groups to serve purposes of their own.

15. We ought to eliminate emissions that rise high in the atmosphere and lead to the deterioration of the ozone layer.

16. Some of the energies that most people now employ to improve their own material status ought instead to be used to help stamp out evil in the world.

You no doubt noticed that virtually every item in the lists above was a *practice,* not a physical object. We can readily supply examples for these lists that are objects, such as:

17. Sulfa drugs ought to exist, because they help save human lives.

18. Crack cocaine ought not to exist, because only evil comes from it.

. . . And so on. The others, however, are more typical of actual speech. This is probably consistent with the idea that it is not the *things* in the world that matter most to us, but the practices we undertake with regard to those things. Moreover, the selection of fairly typical, conversational statements for the lists have determined for us that the items on those lists, with one or two possible exceptions, are not only value claims but *moral* value claims.

Thus we have climbed another flight of our spiral staircase. How do we know what ought to be? Without yet speaking with any finality about it, we can say that we believe it is things like the principles first listed in this chapter. We can guide our conduct by using principles like these, making from them specific judgments having the pattern "Here's what you ought to do" (or "Here's what you ought not to do").

But there are greater heights yet to scale. You probably want your principles to fit into a coherent system brought together by some unifying concept. We'll move farther toward that state in chapter 29, with preparation for it all the way along, and especially in chapters 12, 14, and 27. Keep climbing!

10

Why Classify Statements as Fact- or Value-Claiming?

The preface of this book has already suggested some of the benefits we may receive from knowing about value-claiming statements, and about values themselves. We pointed out there that through an awareness of values and of those statements that say something about values, we will be much better able to assess what people say or write, especially when they are trying to make us believe what they themselves believe. Further, we will be better able to know the nature of our own beliefs, to know exactly which of our beliefs are factual and which are valuative. With this sort of self-knowledge we will be better able to formulate opinions wisely on public issues as well as personal ones, and better able to persuade others to our own views.

These results, however, are brought about partly through a more direct reason we have for separating the fact-claiming from the value-claiming statements.

In chapter 4, there was a demonstration intended to prove the point that no number of believers, no matter how large, is enough by itself to establish that a given proposition is true. Let us suppose that in the year 100 there were a thousand people who believed that the world was flat. Time passed, and by 1492 there were a million people who believed that the world was flat. The impressive increase in numbers would not have been enough to make it suddenly true, in 1492, that the world *was* flat! The number of people believing the proposition "The world is flat" simply had no relation to the actual shape of the world. Now of course we sometimes take the number of persons believing a given proposition to be a *sign* that it is true, but we try to answer the question of whether it is true by other means, not merely by counting votes, and especially not by trying to persuade more and more people to declare belief on a matter they just don't know much about.

Whether the earth is flat is a question whose answer is a fact-claiming statement. That is, it is the case that either "The world is flat" or "The world is not flat." Even the falsity of the answer "The world is flat" doesn't keep it from being fact-*claiming* in nature, though it fails to state a fact. It's "trying to," we might say, and that is enough for it to be fact-claiming, in spite of doing a bad job. In the same way, the statement "The world is round" is also fact-claiming. That one is much closer to the truth than the first one, although geographers will want it to be qualified in certain ways before they could call it true. (They know that the world deviates from the perfect sphere in various ways, such as by its being somewhat flattened at the poles.)

Now, just as a great number of votes does not make a fact-claiming proposition true, neither does a great number of votes make a value-claiming proposition true. In chapter 4, a value-claiming proposition was described as a *matter of opinion.* For such a matter, persons might *agree* upon the proposition, but they have no way to prove it.

The most important reason why it is important to be able to distinguish value-claiming propositions from fact-claiming propositions is simply that, unlike fact-claiming propositions, *all value-claiming propositions are matters of opinion. They can never be proved.*

If it seems at first to you as though this cannot be so, I suggest that you test this statement (yes, it's fact-claiming!) by going back through the book thus far, rereading each value-claiming proposition given, and asking yourself whether the proposition can be tested objectively. I am confident enough of this to say that if you have understood what you have read, you will discover no value judgment that can be proven. You may come to quite a few with which you, or even a majority, would *agree,* but that says nothing about our ability to *prove* them.

If you are still not convinced, make up for yourself a list of value-claiming statements—that is, a list of statements about how the world, in some respect, ought to be, or about what, in some respect, ought to be done. Now submit these to the same test. You may be able to find ways to get people to agree with you; but if you have not put the wrong thing into the list, you will find that the value-claiming statements cannot be proved.

You shouldn't let me go farther without substantiating this drastic claim that I am making. I owe you an explanation of how I know it, or why I believe it. Here it is.

A statement that relates how things *ought to be* has a strong hint of the future about it. If a condition or situation, an "it," isn't a certain way now, the only time "it" can be that way is in the future. "Murchison always ought to sing 'Yankee Doodle' in the key of E flat" gives Murchison only the future in which to do it. "Kenneth ought to stay home and help his mother with the younger children" has the future, and only the future, in which Kenneth can make good on the criticism aimed at him. Even "T. S. Eliot's poetry is the best I've read," although it refers to reading of poetry that I have done in the past, relates to the future because when we utter value judgments we are in effect inviting our listener to agree with us, and the only time in which he can agree—especially if he has to read Eliot's poetry first—is the future.

When we are casting about for value judgments to help us solve our problems, we surely have the future in mind. Here are some slightly modified versions of propositions offered in chapter 4 for solving certain specific problems:

1. I ought to show my wife that I really want to make her happy.

2. I ought to get my son to shift his attention from his bicycle to the things that he should be learning in school.

3. I ought to make sure that fuel is getting to the engine of my lawn mower.

4. Here's what you ought to do.

In each of these examples, it is obvious that relative to the time in which the value judgments are arrived at and stated, the action that will take place to solve these problems is in the future. It is true that some of the value judgments or ought-judgments that we hear (or that we ourselves state) are in the present, or past, or even past perfect tense. But even in those cases, relative to the moment of first deciding upon the judgment, the resolution takes place in the future. Consider the following example:

5. Murchison always sang "Yankee Doodle" in the key of C. He ought to have sung it in the key of E flat.

If Murchison were singing "Yankee Doodle" in the key of C right now, we would admonish him to sing it in E flat right now, and if Murchison thereupon shifted to E flat, it would be after (though ever so slightly) the moment "right now" when we spoke to him, that he made the shift. Similarly, if Murchison had been singing "Yankee Doodle" in C yesterday, and we had admonished him at that time to change, he might have changed key yesterday, but it would have been in the future relative to the moment that he had been singing in C and our subsequent admonition to him to change.

We have six basic tenses in English. They are the present, past, future, present perfect, past perfect, and future perfect. Examples of each, in order, are: "I am playing cards," "I played cards," "I will play cards," "I have played cards," "I had played cards," and "I will have played cards." Each tense has its own moment in past, present, or future time on which its statements are organized, and each such moment has its own past, present, and future. Thus even when we are talking about a time yesterday, say eleven o'clock in the morning, we can still make our statement refer to the future, as of that moment yesterday. (For example, "At eleven o'clock yesterday he did not know that he would be playing cards at noon today.")

It may become a little tricky to see the way in which the simple present-tense value-claiming statements (the ones having the pattern "X is good") look toward the future, but let's try.

In chapter 5 we said that "X is good" means "X is as it ought to be." Then we contrasted the affirmative value-claiming proposition "X is good" with its opposite, "X is not good." We pointed out that if we believed "X is not good," we would be inclined to change X, whereas if we believed "X is good" we were inclined to keep X the same as it is now. So of course if we were going to change X, when we started to change it, it would be in the future relative to the time that we had reached the value judgment, "X is not good."

Thus, when we are driven to say, "These paint brushes are the worst in the world," and set about replacing them, we find the better paint brushes at a moment following that in which we first made the judgment, that is, the moment of finding new brushes is in the future relative to the moment of judging the other brushes to be bad. When we judge, "Tom sings poorly," we change the channel or get up and leave the room, maybe very soon but our action is in the future relative to the moment when we phrased our opinion.

That is how the *negative* present-tense value assertions relate to the future; they make use of the idea of the future to convey their meaning. Now, the *affirmative* present-tense value claims do so in a corresponding way. They hinge on the presumption that when we have adjudged something to be just as it ought to be, we are *not* going to change it. So, when will it stay the same as it is now? In the future, of course.

The upshot of our analysis is this. We test empirical fact-claiming statements by using our senses—we go and look (or we listen, or we sniff, or we lift, or whatever is appropriate). We test our logical and mathematical fact-claiming statements by seeking and examining the relations among ideas. Thus all the factual statements have a realm to which we may give our attention when we want to find out whether they are true. But nothing of the sort can be done for the value-claiming propositions. Their realm is that of the future, and the future simply hasn't gotten here yet. So there's no place to look.

That is why you cannot test an *ought*-judgment, a value-claiming proposition, in any objective way. As a consequence, the value-claiming propositions simply do not have the dimension of truth or falsity. Fact-claiming propositions have that dimension. But they get it at the cost of being unable to tell us what the future ought to be like, what ought to be done, what conditions ought to be brought about. Each kind of statement has its advantages, and its limitations.

Now you know what kind of statement may by its nature be susceptible of proof (the fact-claiming statements), and what kind can never be proved (the value-claiming statements). This information is of the greatest importance when appraising someone's arguments, wondering whether or not to believe his conclusions.

Truth belongs to the fact-claiming propositions. What belongs to the value-claiming propositions, in place of truth? It is *wisdom,* the ability to make excellent value judgments.

What are excellent value judgments? We will try to answer that question in chapter 27.

11

How *Ought* Is Used

The word *ought* is apparently an early form of *owed,* the perfect passive participle of the verb *owe.* There is a difference, however, from its simply being an equivalent of *owed.* The difference is that we nowadays ordinarily use *owe* having in mind an indirect object, a word or phrase indicating a person or thing to whom something is owed, whereas we use *ought* more abstractly. We use it cut loose, as it were, from the specifying of a person or other being to whom something is owed.

When we are using the word *owe* in the conventional way, we are following a pattern like this one:

I owe *X* to *A.*

That could be "I owe twenty dollars to my brother," or "I owe my parents a letter," or "He owes his employees an explanation." Each of these can be transformed into a sentence using *ought*: "I ought to pay my brother twenty dollars," "I ought to write my parents a letter," "He ought to explain to his employees." These expressions keep the indirect object—the beneficiary, we might call it—of the obligation that is expressed. Moreover, expressions like these are so numerous that we tend strongly to associate the idea of *obligation* with the word *ought.*

However, numerous other propositions using *ought* do not express a relationship to a specific beneficiary. Some examples are:

1. I ought to pay my debts.

2. I ought to keep up with my correspondence.

3. He ought to keep the lines of communication open.

When we look at these, we can take cues from their content to suggest who the beneficiaries are. In the first example it is all the people to whom I owe money. In the second it is all the people to whom I owe letters. And in the third it is anybody to whom "he" ought to pass information. Though we may accurately figure out who the beneficiary would be, it gets less definite who that is as our list continues.

4. He ought to give some of his money to charity.

5. She ought to show more respect for the dead.

6. There is a general rule under which any act falls, and everyone ought to conduct him/herself in such a way that he or she could exert an act of will making that general rule apply not only to him/herself but to everyone.

7. She ought to do everything consistently with what the Bible teaches.

8. He always ought to do whatever will bring him the greatest pleasure.

With these examples, we are moving away from the idea of there being a particular beneficiary of the obligation borne. Take the fourth example: Does the subject *owe* money to charity? If so, which charity? *All* charities? Does he owe it to one charity that he should give money to some other charity? The specifying of a beneficiary is so vague in these examples that if we insist on there being one, it gets in the way of our understanding what is being expressed in the value claim. To understand the judgment, it is better not to think in terms of any particular beneficiary.

Look at the fifth example: To whom does the subject owe more respect for the dead? To the dead themselves? *All* of them? Who even knows how many dead there are? Or does she owe it to the rest of the living—all of *them*? Nobody really knows how many of them there are either. To *both* all of the dead *and* all of the living? One couldn't have a broader obligation than that, eh? It is simply not practical to attempt to pin down the beneficiary to whom this obligation is owed.

The sixth example expresses in everyday language a principle of conduct formulated by the German philosopher Immanuel Kant, in an effort to show that the sheer logic of reason imposes an obligation upon a person to act with moral correctness. The seventh example gives little indication of the person to whom the subject is obliged to act in the way suggested, and if we propose "God," we are adding a new idea that isn't present in the assertion itself. The eight example expresses hedonism, a belief that some will say assumes an obligation to the individual who is spoken about, while others will retort that it is a belief in no obligation at all, but just a recognition of selfishness.

Thus we see that, whether or not you happen to agree with any of these expressions, the idea of *owing,* as in "I owe *X* to *A,*" can actually function without the "to *A,*" and becomes a more abstract idea, less focused on a specific individual to whom the benefit of the obligation might be paid. It becomes a generalized duty, perhaps involving all the living and the dead who have preceded them—and the future generations as well. This appears to be what is involved in the more general statements that use *ought* rather than *owe* to make their point. Indeed, *ought* has become virtually autonomous, and when people use it they rarely think in terms of owing anything to anyone in particular.

Here are some further examples of the use of *ought* with its usual broad scope.

9. One ought never to take a human life.

10. One ought never to leave a child unattended in the presence of great danger.

11. One ought always to help the weak, sick, or disabled, when they are unable to help themselves.

12. One ought to develop one's talents and capabilities to the greatest possible extent.

13. Harry ought to try to act less like a fool.

14. The president ought to listen to the voice of the common people.

15. America ought to be a world leader in efforts toward peace.

In some of these examples you may think in terms of a beneficiary, but it is not necessary to have one to understand what is said. The fact that the beneficiary is left open also leaves open the possibility that there might not be a specific beneficiary at all; that there could be such a thing as conduct that is obligated, but not obligated toward any certain person or persons.

It is especially needful to understand that *ought*-judgments may be made, and be worthy of our full attention, in the absence of any certain party who is to get the benefit of them. Such *ought*-judgments are important factors in what we call the moral life, in the morality of relations among persons. We will look further at some of these factors at the beginning of the next chapter.

12

Kinds of Ought

Philosophers who are interested in the theory of value recognize and study several kinds of *ought*-judgment (that is, value claims using the word *ought*). Thus they divide the realm of the *ought* into branches. I should like to identify five of these branches, while conceding that there might be others. Here I'll give samples of *ought*-judgments from each branch, followed by an explanation distinguishing that branch from others.

THE MORAL OUGHT

1. You ought to pay your freely contracted debts.

2. You ought not to rip off the power company by wiring in a by-pass around your electric meter.

3. Bill Sawyer ought to contribute some of his money to the charities that supply food to the homeless.

4. You ought to treat every other person as your equal in personhood, even if he or she is not your equal in wealth or good looks or intelligence.

5. Every healthy citizen ought to donate his organs, upon death, to those whose health can be restored through organ transplants.

6. We all ought to do everything we can to promote peace.

7. Authors ought never to incorporate into their writing any passages written by someone else without giving full and correct credit to the other author and the copyright owner.

8. One ought to live one's life in such a way as to bring about the least possible harm and the most possible good to others.

9. That angry father ought not to have used an iron pipe to spank his child.

10. In speaking about one's future actions, one ought to make a clear distinction between what one actually promises and what is merely a general intention.

The value claims of the above list are all examples of moral *ought*-judgments. In the philosophical field of ethics, the word *ought* is used to signify obligation, so that "you ought to" is taken to mean "you have an obligation to." There is much debate about when and toward whom an obligation exists. Some moral philosophers seem to leave little else in ethics or morality besides obligation and its implications. To commit a moral wrong, for them, is to violate an obligation.

In our present study, we need not pursue the questions of where obligation comes from or what its nature is. Rather we should acknowledge that moral *ought*-judgments are about actions in relations between persons regarded as *moral agents,* which is to say, persons who can do right or wrong. These may be relations of oneself with another individual or with a group of other individuals, or between other individuals and groups not including oneself, or between oneself and society. Moral judgments can pertain to an individual, to a group of any size, even to the whole world, now and always.

THE AESTHETIC OUGHT

1. A painter, when composing a picture, ought to place the chief elements in the pattern of a simple common and well known geometric form, such as a triangle, a square, or a cross.

2. A novel ought to get under way with a conflict between characters, the nearer to the opening page the better.

3. His novel ought to have had a more convincing portrayal of the home life of the quarreling characters.

4. A composer ought never to forget that a part of the power of instrumental music comes from the analogy of the instrument to the human voice.

5. The director ought not to have let his actors maintain such a high emotional pitch throughout the first act.

6. This poet ought to strive to reach a more fundamental level of human experience, in at least some of his poems.

7. You ought to wear that outfit more often, because it's very becoming to you.

Aesthetic statements relate to beauty and that which looks or sounds attractive (as well as their opposites, the ugly and the unattractive), and in general to the arts. These examples deal with painting, literature, drama or film, music, and costume for everyday or special occasions. Most of those who are familiar with aesthetic matters will, I think, agree that choosing colors for one's costume can be truly an aesthetic consideration. Such matters are often called "matters of taste," and in these things we are often reminded that there is no proving the deliverances about taste by this or that individual.

An important group of aesthetic *ought*-judgments is neither spoken nor written, and perhaps cannot be said in words. These are the judgments made in the mind of the creative artist as he is doing his work: "What shall I put *here*? It ought to be a piece of furniture. What should be the tone of this next addition? It ought to be receding rather than conspicuous." And so on.

Next in frequency among aesthetic judgments are probably the judgments of spectators, such as "Katharine Hepburn's performance in *On Golden Pond* was beautiful," or, in our explanatory translation, "Katharine Hepburn's performance in *On Golden Pond* was just as it ought to be." (This is closer to our basic rendition of "is good" and other valuative predicates; it lacks the imperative sound of the "you ought to . . . ," "someone ought to . . ." of the sample moral *ought*-judgments given above.)

The phrase *aesthetic judgment,* however, is not normally used by philosophers and critics to identify individual propositions. Rather, it is usually intended to name the faculty or ability or practice of doing the kind of deciding through which we generally characterize works of art or natural phenomena when considered as aesthetic presentations. I have to admit, therefore, that my discussion of the aesthetic *ought* speaks of something less essential than what most aestheticians will think of when the phrase *aesthetic judgment* is used.

THE RELIGIOUS *OUGHT*

1. You ought to love, revere, and respect your God.

2. You ought to consider every action or every abstention from action as though your salvation depended on it.

3. You ought not to let a day go by without offering up a prayer.

4. You ought to worship only the Creator and not the thing created.

5. You ought not to use the name of God as part of an expression of displeasure or in any other way than worshipfully.

6. Even though you have an opportunity to offend without being detected by other people, you ought to hold yourself accountable to the Deity for your actions.

Although the second sample is evidently offered within a Christian context and may not be espoused as widely as the others, all the statements have to do not with the individual's relation to other human persons but rather to his deity.

Religious *ought*-judgments derive, at least in part, from the beliefs of the individual as handed down by his religious organization. Some religious denominations place the whole field of morals within the larger field of religion, making all moral judgments also religious judgments, and for the most part construing moral infractions as offenses against the divine as well as against a human party.

The great variety of creeds in the world makes it difficult to speak both generally and at the same time accurately about religious *ought*-statements. What holds true of one religion is in many instances contradicted or contested by another. Perhaps each reader will improve on the above list by supplying additional *ought*-judgments from his own body of religious belief.

THE PRUDENTIAL OUGHT

1. Martha ought to take most of her money out of those low-paying certificates of deposit and put it into something that produces more income, like mutual funds that invest in bonds.

2. You'd better take your umbrella when you go out, Henry!

3. You ought not to have such long, dangling shoelaces, because you'll trip on them.

4. You ought to save some of your money, even though you earn so little.

5. You may feel healthy, but since your feet are giving you a good deal of trouble you ought to go to a doctor.

6. I have so many books now that I ought to put them on the shelves in alphabetical order by author.

7. I ought to go to the bank and get out some money before I leave on my trip this weekend.

8. You ought to brush your teeth before you go out—unless you plan to sit on the other end of the sofa from your date.

9. The store ought to light these shelves better, so people can pick out their sprinkler system parts more easily.

The branch of *ought*-judgments which I call prudential is not very much touched upon by the philosophers, probably because they do not see very many general problems that it raises. These judgments are simply those relating to the self-interest of an individual in carrying on his life. It is prudent to take good care of one's health, to preserve and increase one's share of worldly goods, to develop one's pleasure-yielding talents, and so on.

Occasionally self-interested judgments are contrasted with altruistic judgments, relating them in that way to reasoning about ethics or morals.

THE *OUGHT* OF TRADITION, ETIQUETTE, AND MANNERS

1. When setting the table, one should put the knife and spoon on the right hand side of the plate, and the fork on the left hand side.

2. Galt should have waited until his hostess had sat down, before he sat down himself.

3. Mondschein ought to wear a tie when he is at his office.

4. When you call someone on the phone, you should always give your name before entering into conversation.

5. When you go to visit Haru Okosu at his home, and are invited in, you should always remove your shoes before entering.

The value-claiming statements we encounter in this group are those that stem from good manners and from traditional forms of clothing, behavior, and so on. To many, this field of *ought*-judgments seems of little importance while others regard it as all-important.

The significance of these categories, these branches of value theory, lies in the answer to the question "How do you know what ought to be?" This question is fundamental in giving order to one's personal conduct or to that of one's group, nation, or society. Yet its final answer is not obvious.

For our immediate purposes, perhaps even our medium long-range purposes, we can give some answers. Chapter 7 suggested the pattern we follow to respond to problems as they arise: We solve them by referring to some general rule that we know, some principle, under which our problem falls. Thus we make a specific value judgment to guide our immediate conduct. Chapter 9 listed seven principles—a far from exhaustive list; there are many more!—that we use, to reflect upon more challenging problems. They are not final answers in themselves, because they are open to conflicting, even contradictory, interpretations for specific cases; and in some instances more than one seems to apply to a case, so that we need to prioritize them to reach our applicable value judgment.

The hardest problems are those of the moral sphere. Certainly the most difficult task in validating or justifying decisions resulting in value judgments relates to moral value judgments. For the time being, let us say that the way you know what ought to be, including what ought or ought not to be done, is by consulting your moral code, thinking earnestly and thoroughly about what it tells you and applying it stringently to your problem.

And where do you obtain your moral code? Different persons receive theirs from different places. Some depend upon religion; others upon the family; others upon their schools; others on institutions, such as the Boy Scouts and the Girl Scouts, the YMCA/YWCA, or other character-forming organizations; others on a code of ethics of their profession or occupation; still others upon what they find in their culture. Some persons have at some stage of their life diverged from a previously accepted source of a moral code and have vowed to construct one of their own.

In matters of beauty and the arts, the source of justification for one's judgments is usually one's education and upbringing, so far as it has touched upon these subjects. Often, however, we are left on our own in such matters and simply develop criteria of our own. The well-known saying, "I don't know anything about art, but I know what I like," probably reflects this situation.

As to religious duties or instructions, these usually derive from the religion in which a person was raised. After instruction and learning at home, he or she may undergo further instruction at a church, synagogue, or other religious site. Many, however, change their religious commitments, perhaps more than once, during their life. One is ordinarily called upon to make religious value judgments especially in bringing up one's children, and usually turns to one's religion for authority in these matters.

Regarding our prudential judgments, the world is strident with advice about what we ought to be and do. Every advertisement, every self-help book or magazine article, every TV commercial, and even many well-intentioned conversations are full of somebody's opinion of what is good for each of us. We spend considerable time during our lives in separating out the good advice from the noise.

We first learn the traditional rules and patterns of conduct of our society through our parents and families, our schooling, and similar experiences. Various institutions have traditions of their own and expect conformity to them: the military services, clubs, fraternities and sororities, vocations, and professions. These may even publish printed versions of their codes. Those regarded as authorities publish books on manners and etiquette, advice on personal relationships, and explanations of our customs. One may refer to these guide books and books of rules and etiquette, not to mention the advice columnists, for information on the code under which one is expected to act.

The important thing about knowing what sort of classification a value judgment belongs to is not merely the ability to allot it unequivocally to one or another category, but an idea of where to look for help in considering whether it should be accepted or rejected. As a matter of fact, a given value judgment might belong in each of two or more categories. Consider this first example:

1. You ought never to wear a brown business suit.

At the time this advice is spoken, brown business suits are out of favor in the business and fashion worlds. We could decide that this example belongs among the fashion rules within the category of tradition, a traditional *ought*-judgment, because it is about a color of clothing. But we could also decide that it is a prudential judgment, because (horrors!) the wearer of a brown business suit will be looked down upon by those with whom he attempts to do business. Still again, we might consider it an aesthetic judgment, if it is apparently made on grounds of taste (for example, if brown is a very unbecoming color to the individual concerned).

Quite possibly a certain office worker would have no objection of his own to wearing a brown business suit, but won't wear one because he knows they are out of fashion and therefore his co-workers would think less of him for wearing one—something he does not want for reasons of success in his work. Thus the judgment is both prudential and aesthetic, as well as a judgment about fashion.

Yes, a value judgment might represent *three* branches of value theory. The following example does as well:

2. It is certainly in bad taste for this guest of the college to sit at the president's table and complain about the president's wife's recent activism on behalf of the local district teachers.

This example expresses a moral judgment, since the speaker is saying that the guest's complaint is injurious to both the president and his wife. It is also an aesthetic judgment, for which the tip-off is the phrase "bad taste," showing that its speaker considers the conduct concerned to be rather more ugly than attractive. Finally, it is a breach of good manners, under a widespread code of manners that calls for dinner-table conversation to be convivial for anyone present, and also calls for preserving a pleasant atmosphere when one is a guest.

Here is another example, with a variation—it belongs in two branches, but it belongs in one of them for more than one reason:

3. Drivers ought not to drive at speeds above sixty-five miles per
   hour on the interstate highways.

This proposition is a moral *ought*-judgment, because it deals
with the right and wrong of relations among moral agents—a driver, other drivers on the road, the law enforcement officers, and
the general public, whose highways are involved. It is also a prudential judgment, for two reasons. One is that a driver exceeding
the speed limit is liable to be arrested and fined; no reasonable
driver wants that. The other is that authorities have deemed speeds
higher than the posted limit to greatly increase the likelihood of an
accident, and no reasonable driver wants an accident either. Thus
there are two ways it is good for him to stay at or below sixty-five,
and two ways it could be bad for him not to.

In the area of value inquiry as well as in many other important
areas, especially the humane and social disciplines, it is rare to be
able to keep categories and classifications pure and clear. A moral
ought-judgment may have close connection with an aesthetic one,
or a prudential *ought*-judgment with a moral one. Other combinations often occur. It is helpful to be able to single out the categories of judgment that are involved so we can know what kind of
justifying principles to seek, and along with that to clarify discussion and debate over justifications of the judgment.

Value judgments are not part of a vast, cohesive system.
Rather, they are generated freely by individuals as they see fit.
Consequently value judgments can be in conflict with one another,
just as persons can. Sometimes one and the same person entertains
two value judgments that collide, and so has to work out his own
resolution of the conflict. See the next example:

4. City law rightly forbids Marilyn Pardee from dancing nude in
   bars, even though her beauty, if anyone's, is great enough to
   justify the nude dance.

The speaker utters two value judgments in these clauses. First, he says, it is right, as the city law provides, that there should be no nude dancing in the city's bars; second, Marilyn Pardee's beauty is great enough to justify nude dancing. With his "even though," the speaker places his moral approval of the law above his aesthetic appreciation of Marilyn Pardee and the dance she performs. This suggests that the speaker of the fourth example gives all moral *ought*-judgments a higher place than aesthetic ones. It helps him to know the categories of value claims, because it makes him able, if he wishes, to place certain whole categories above others.

Of course, not everyone would put the two judgments in that order. How would you reason, in order to decide which should outweigh the other? Some persons would appeal to religion, and thus bring *three* branches of value theory into the fray!

13

Recognizing Value Judgments in Specific Cases

In your critical thinking about events in your private life or in public life, there are four situations in which value judgments are especially important. These occur:

1. *When you are reading the writing of other persons or listening to them speaking.* They may spend much of their discourse giving you information, and they may or may not give you some of their value judgments along with that information. You will want to be able to recognize any value judgments that are scattered among their fact-claiming statements, as well as to recognize whether their conclusion (if any) is value-claiming, and to keep these value claims separate in your mind from the factual statements. Each of the two types, you recall, has its own separate method of support.

2. *When you are shaping your own thoughts for your own benefit.* You need to be able to recognize which of your thoughts are fact-

claiming and which are value-claiming. Since this sort of study is new, the schools have not as yet paid much attention to it. Accordingly, most of us grow up without even knowing which of our thoughts are value-claiming, and how they relate to those that are fact-claiming. This book is an attempt to catch up.

3. *When someone is putting his own value claims before you and trying to get you to believe them.* People offer an *argument,* a set of chosen reasons, designed to convince you of what they want you to believe. You will want to know whether you should believe the value claims, and to get to that point you will want to know how good the other person's arguments are. Therefore, you will want to know how to evaluate those arguments.

4. *When you want to persuade someone else,* perhaps large numbers of people, to accept *your* value judgments. You will want to know how value judgments can be supported, and how they cannot.

If people would make sure that all their expressed value judgments used the word *ought,* it would be easy to distinguish between fact-claiming and value-claiming statements—but our language would lose much of its richness. It is more practical, very useful, and indeed fairly easy for us to identify value claims by applying our key question to statements we are interested in. The key question is, "What does the statement relate—the way it *is,* or the way it *ought to be?*" It is important to be aware of the statements that embody a value judgment, because we want to know which statements can be proved and which cannot.

Let us now look at some examples that are drawn from daily life or encountered in readily accessible reading matter, and consider how they express value judgments even though the word *ought* does not occur.

1. I must write my will one day soon.

This is value-claiming, since it states "what I ought to do." But contrast the *must* her with the *must* in "Since he left at eight o'clock this morning, he must be in Tokyo by now." That sentence is fact-claiming. The meaning of *must* in each sentence is quite different. Therefore, we cannot regard the word as a sure sign either of a value claim or a factual statement. Rather, we apply our question, and realize that the speaker is stating what in his view ought to be, namely, that if things were the way they ought to be, he would be writing his will. (In the Tokyo example, *must* means "It is reasonable to infer that . . .")

2. It's time we got out of stocks and into bonds.

Here we clearly have a value claim: "We *ought to* get out of stocks and into bonds." It would be better, the statement says, for us to change our holdings from stocks to bonds. The reference to time means "now," or may more vaguely mean "while conditions in the economy are the way they are." However, in a different context, the mention of time could be primary in the sentence and could make it a statement of fact, as for example in "It's time to get up. The alarm clock has just rung." This statement simply tells what time it is. The value judgment of when to set the alarm clock was already made the evening before, when someone set the alarm.

3. Regrettably, George continued to scold the child long after her remorseful tears were dry.

The word *regrettably,* starting off this sentence and applying to its whole idea, is a value-judgmental word. It assumes someone's viewpoint—that of the speaker, that of an outside observer, possibly even that of George himself—and indicates "not as it ought to be" from that viewpoint. The rest of the sentence is quite factual, but the strongest idea is that George's continued scolding is something that ought not to be.

4. A bumper sticker reading: HATE is not a family value.

Here is a clear value claim. To classify something in our present-day society as a "family value" is to say that it is as it ought to be, and this statement denies that status to hate. Hence it means "Hate is not as it ought to be," or more broadly, "There ought to be no hate."

5. From *The Hope* by Herman Wouk:

> "I received yesterday," Moshe Dayan put in, "a copy of an article by the British expert Liddell Hart on our campaign. He calls it 'a classic of the military art.' "[1]

Let's condense the statement to: "The Israeli campaign was a classic of the military art."

In virtually every context or situation, to classify something as "a classic" of "an art" is to affirm that it is as it ought to be. The conventional impression of what a classic is, is that it is something that is especially, or in a high degree, as it ought to be.

6. You'd better not leave those candles so near the stove.

Here *better* functions as a signal word, identifying a value assertion. "You'd better not" says "you ought not." It compares leaving the candles near the stove and removing them to a place farther from the stove, and says that the latter is more as it ought to be than the former.

7. "The interest of the patient is the only interest to be considered."—Dr. Will Mayo.[2]

The sense of this statement is, "The interest of the patient *ought to be* the only interest to be considered." The device of forming a value claim in the pattern of a factual claim is a way well known to writers and speakers for making value judgments especially forceful and believable. See the following example.

8. A Scout is trustworthy, loyal, helpful, friendly, courteous, kind, obedient, cheerful, thrifty, brave, clean, and reverent.

Undoubtedly there are Scouts who can be described by all of these adjectives. But for those at whom it is aimed, namely, boys who are interested in becoming Scouts, its force is value-assertive. They are being told that a Scout *ought to be* trustworthy, loyal, and so on. Here, too, we see a value claim in the guise of a statement of fact.

9. From a newspaper article by David S. Broder:

> Loss of confidence in representative government is a bigger threat to this country than approval or rejection of NAFTA [the North American Free Trade Agreement]. The press that hyped the [Al] Gore-[Ross] Perot show and ignored [Phil] Gramm and [Richard] Gephardt (who actually will cast votes on the issue) needs to reexamine its values.[3]

The first sentence in this paragraph, concluding one of Broder's editorial columns, is a *factual claim* of a widely encountered kind. On the assumption that threats can be measured (as small, medium, and large), we can confidently call this sentence a fact claim. It is "telling it the way it is," in Broder's opinion, and there is nothing in it to indicate to us what—again, in Broder's opinion—is the way things ought to be. This first statement is a matter of opinion and would be difficult to prove, but it is a matter of *factual* rather than valuative opinion. The reader's experience might support it, and if so he might consider the statement proved.

But the second sentence gives us some idea of what Broder thinks is the way it ought to be. Ought the press give a high-pressure buildup to the Al Gore-Ross Perot debate and soft-pedal the Phil Gramm-Richard Gephardt debate? No—the press that did that "needs to reexamine its values." This surely tells us that Broder judges that a certain segment of the press *ought* to have given major attention to the Gramm-Gephardt debate, more emphasis than it did to the Gore-Perot debate. Thus the second sentence is about what ought to be, and (again, even though the reader might agree) cannot be proved.

10. "Seriousness, community, ritual—these are values that help give civility its life. We must recapture them."[4]

In saying that seriousness, community, and ritual are values, this author is in fact making a value judgment upon each of the three, saying that each ought to be present in civil life. Then with "We *must* recapture them," he is telling us what we ought to do. (Compare with the first example.) Both sentences express value judgments.

But not every statement that contains the word *value* (or its plural, *values*) is necessarily a value claim. The statement, "The 1992 presidential election campaign was fought largely on issues of values" is fact-claiming. It gives not even a hint about how things ought to be, in the writer's view, but only about how he perceived the events of the campaign. Once again, we need to refer to our question "What does the statement relate—the way it *is,* or the way it *ought to be?*"

11. The body is the temple of the soul.

To analyze this statement, we ask what appears to be its purpose, or its general effect. What factual information does it carry? Practically speaking, none. Then what use is it? Well, it makes one respect the body by associating it with the soul, for which we tend to have great respect. We also tend to respect temples and to value them. Thus the statement is a way of saying that the body is good, is as it ought to be. The sentence can be applied to discourses urging that the body be respected, cared for, and not mistreated through, for example, drug abuse. This statement, of course, is a figure of speech, a metaphor, not intended literally. Thus, as it expresses no literal factual information but rather a strong view that the body ought to be revered, the sentence is a value claim.

NOTES

1. Herman Wouk, *The Hope* (Boston: Little, Brown & Co., 1993), p. 317.

2. Wall motto, main lobby of Mayo Clinic Jacksonville, Jacksonville, Florida.

3. David S. Broder, "Capital Politics: The Wrong Debate," *Washington Post National Weekly Edition,* November 15–23, 1993, p. 4.

4. Ivan Strenski, "Recapturing the Values That Promote Civility on the Campuses," *Chronicle of Higher Education,* June 23, 1993, p. A36.

14

Knowing Your Own Mind: Recognizing Your Own Value Judgments

"I don't know anything about art, but I know what I like!" This well-known remark can typify for us the frame of mind of the person who needs to become able to recognize and express his own value judgments. It is often offered as a mockery of the person who has no education in art but is loud and cocksure about what he thinks of certain artworks. But the saying can again speak for the art fan who believes that we don't have to have a great deal of historical or technical knowledge about the arts, so long as we are willing to develop our own tastes. In either case, we can let the statement remind us that there are indeed those who do not know what their own value judgments are, or what these would be if they had any, independently of the emotion of liking—which you and I now know is *not* the fundamental basis of valuation.

There really are, then, times when a person doesn't know what his own valuation is, or what his own value judgments are. Few of us are habitually reflective thinkers, constantly shaping and honing our own thoughts. For this, and perhaps other, reasons, we are occasionally stumped when someone asks us, for example, "What do *you* think of the Russo-Latvian situation?" We realize that there *is* a Russo-Latvian situation, but have not decided on any of its pros or cons. So we suddenly have to tie a shoelace and let someone else speak, until we hear something we can contradict. A Midwestern lady is reported to have said to Adlai Stevenson when the latter was campaigning for president, "Why, I never know what I think until I hear myself saying it!" Let's illustrate further with the following cases.

CASE 1

Carey and Jeanne, having coffee in their company's canteen, were reacting to an item in the day's news, in which a devotee of a Middle-Eastern religion had planted a bomb in a Manhattan religious bookstore, where he was sure death would result for a huge number of followers of a rival religion.

Carey said, "He took out four of them, plus any of the injured who may yet die."

Jeanne replied, "Not much of a score, considering the possibilities. Why, if an American were to try such an atrocious thing, he would have carried off at least fifty, if not a hundred."

Carey: "That's a strange way to look at it! What makes you so sure?"

Jeanne: "Why, we do everything better than those fellows do. When it comes to anything as intricate as planting a bomb, they're all thumbs. They just don't have the mechanical aptitude that we have."

Carey decides to bait Jeanne: "Really! And how do you know so much about their mechanical aptitude?"

Jeanne: "My uncle lived in their country for several years, and he told me. They can hardly screw in a light bulb, he says. And that fits right in with their general inferiority."

Carey: "Oh, their *general inferiority,* is it? Tell me about that."

Jeanne: "Well, you *know* they're inferior. Did any of 'em ever become a great inventor? Or a great musician? Or a great *anything* that you've ever heard of? You *know* their whole culture is just inferior to ours."

Carey: "What do you mean, I *'know'* it? I don't know it at all!"

Jeanne: "Why, sure you do, Carey! *Everybody* knows it. Just ask anybody."

Carey: "No, I don't take 'anybody' as my authority on what to believe."

Jeanne: "Well, just take yourself, then. Don't you just see it, that that group is inferior? Where are their great physicians, or painters, or for that matter, football or baseball players?"

Carey: "No, I can't see it at all. And it's a point that can't be proven, because it's a value judgment. You are just making a value judgment that one culture is superior to another, and there's no way you can prove a value judgment."

Jeanne: "What do you mean, I can't prove it? I've believed it all my life!"

Carey: "Yes, you can *believe* it, but that doesn't prove it. And you can 'ask anybody,' but no matter how many agree, that doesn't prove it. You have to realize that, after all, it's only a value judgment."

Jeanne: "You mean I've been believing a value judgment all my life, and I can't prove it?"

Carey: "Yes, you're just like M. Jourdain, the character in Molière's play, who's been speaking prose all his life, but never knew it."

At this point Carey explains to Jeanne what value judgments are, and why it is that they cannot be proven. Jeanne has learned that one of her firm beliefs is a value judgment, and now she is on

the way to being able to identify other value judgments among her
beliefs. She will be wary, from now on, about claiming truth for
her value claims. Possibly, she will even resolve to try to achieve
wisdom in making them.

Let's work out a few ways in which individuals might avoid
being left in such unsteady positions as Jeanne's.

CASE 2

Paul Proctor is a college freshman. He has been assigned to write
a brief essay for his political science class affirming his position
on whether the recent election for governor in his state was a fair
one. Paul decides to use a method that he had been taught in his
freshman composition class and his speech communication class,
which is sometimes called *brainstorming*. You write down many
ideas, as fast as you can, and don't worry about what they say so
long as they have to do with your topic (here, fairness in the recent election). Then when you run out of things to say, you look
over the accumulation and see whether a conclusion emerges.

After doing considerable background reading, Paul sets many
facts down on a sheet, then a second sheet, of paper. The election
was on a Tuesday, the polls were open from 7 A.M. to 7 P.M., a
statewide civic club provided free transportation to the polls, and
so on—a list of facts that seemed to call for a judgment that the
election was fair. But then some factual claims of a different tendency find their way into Paul's paper: The incumbent, who won,
spent sixteen million dollars campaigning and the loser only one
million; the winner had 30-second sound bites every half hour for
two weeks during prime time on all TV channels in the state,
while the loser could afford only 15-second radio sound bites at
the end of the daily livestock price reports; the winner had the ben-

efit of four Hollywood costume and makeup experts and a speech coach, and the loser, none. Finally Paul Proctor decides that the election, even though scrupulously legal, was unfair because the winner had far greater access to money than the challenger.

Paul writes his conclusion: "Thus, while neither candidate broke any election laws, and the election was conducted legally, the economic realities of the situation gave the incumbent candidate a wholly unfair advantage. It wasn't the challenger's fault that he was not a wealthy person."

Each of these two sentences is a value assertion and a moral judgment. Working on the assignment, writing down his thoughts, has helped Paul to come to know what his value judgments are about this election.

CASE 3

Ella lived in a house of her own in a modest neighborhood. She got along well with all her neighbors and knew Marie, who lived next door, very well. Both she and Marie worked for a living. For Marie this was harder than for Ella, because Marie had two small children, and her husband had deserted her when the second was a baby.

Ella was proud that she worked at a steady job, was well thought of by her boss, and managed to save a little bit every month out of her wages. She disdained people who were on welfare, because she considered them lazy and sometimes worse—chiselers and moochers who would rather live on the taxpayers than work.

Marie thought her job was something she could count on. She often listened to Ella complain about the "welfare moochers." She agreed that people who did not want to work but would rather live on public money were lazy.

Then for Marie disaster struck. The company for which she worked declared bankruptcy and went out of business; her job was gone. She did not tell Ella or any other neighbors, but they suspected what had happened because they began seeing Marie at times when she used to be working.

One evening Marie asked Ella to come over and see her. Did Ella, Marie asked, think it would be a totally vile and malingering thing if she went on welfare to feed her children while she was unemployed? It had been nearly the required thirteen consecutive weeks of unemployment and she had to make up her mind.

Ella was flabbergasted, but she said to Marie, "Why of course not! You owe it to your children! I may have said some harsh things about people on welfare, but I only meant the ones who are lazy and want to be freeloaders. I know that you'd rather be working, and welfare was meant for people like you, who really want to work but have to live while they're between jobs. It would be right for you to go on welfare."

Thus Ella found out that she believed down deep that it was right for honest people who were temporarily down and out to go on welfare if they had to. Marie's case let Ella know that some welfare recipients were eager to work but were caught in a bind, and this helped Ella refine her judgment about which welfare allocations she could approve of, and which she could not. Ella did not "brainstorm," but rather "talked it out" with her friend Marie, a pattern many of us follow to get more settled in our own thinking.

CASE 4

Brooks and West regularly meet at a neighborhood sports bar. This evening they are watching TV highlights of great plays from the football season just past. Each has a favorite player.

Brooks: "Winchester is a better football player than Bromwich."

West: "Not on your life! Bromwich is a football player's football player. He's really good even though he isn't very conspicuous on the field."

Brooks: "You're just proving what I'm saying. The guys who are conspicuous on the field are the guys who score and pick up yardage. And Winchester has scored 66 points this season, but Bromwich has only scored 12."

West: "Well, make up your mind. Which is it, points or yardage? I'll take yardage. And Bromwich has picked up 585 yards, but Winchester has only gained 218. All Winchester knows how to do is catch passes."

There's a familiar problem here. Let's get to work on it.

"Winchester is a better football player than Bromwich" is clearly a value-claiming proposition, in one of the classic patterns. The next statement is not in a classic form at all: "Bromwich is a football player's football player" is indeed a value-claiming proposition, but instead of *good, better,* or *best,* it uses an idiomatic expression, "a football player's football player," to express "as a football player ought to be"—even further, "as a football player would judge that a football player ought to be."

Plainly there's a difference of opinion between the two speakers, a difference in value judgment. But the difference may not be about what they think it is!

Brooks begins to realize that some factual details may help him strengthen his argument, so he injects the scoring record of each football player into the discussion. It is obvious to both Brooks and West that 66 is more points than 12.

But West not only comes back with some numbers that favor his own man; he also points out that *an individual may make his own choice of a criterion* for resolving the question of which of two players is better. "I'll take yardage" is his way of announcing his own choice. He believes that a player who gains a superior number of yards in a season is more as a football player ought to be than one who achieves a high number of scored points.

Thus Brooks and West agree that Winchester scored more points than Bromwich, and that Bromwich gained more yards than Winchester. What they disagree on is the relation of these facts to the idea of a football player who is as a football player ought to be. Apparently Brooks believes that a player who scores many points is that kind of player, while West believes that it is one with the ability to gain yards, apart from scoring points. This boils down to Brooks's belief that "points scored are better than yards gained," and West's belief that "yards gained are better than points scored," in measuring the quality of a football player. This is their real disagreement. Evaluating the two football players was rather incidental to it. Their discussion has enabled each one to put into words his value judgment on whether making yardage or scoring points is better football playing.

An important idea emerges from this conversation and its analysis. It is open to anyone who is interested in such a pursuit as football to make his own judgments about the ranking of different aspects of the game. Brooks and West are likely never to agree on the choice of a criterion, and each is entitled to believe as he does. The same is true of pursuing the game of life.

The two methods of identifying one's own value judgments presented thus far are "brainstorming" and "talking it out." Another may be more successful, but is difficult to present by example. It is *reflection*. Simply by asking questions like "What do I really believe?" you can often "pin yourself down" and put into words— value claims—the beliefs that you discover underlying various decisions and attitudes. For those with more practice, this inner dialogue can be quite systematic. The more imaginative you are at putting questions to yourself, the more likely is the session to result in well-formulated, fundamental, and comprehensive answers.

A good place to begin, both to get practice and to help your life on its way, is with value claims that you deny. Someone takes a stand, let us say, on suicide committed by those with incurable and extremely painful illnesses. You disagree. But what, exactly, do you believe in contrast to that person's opinion? A careful and disciplined answer, worked out as a well-phrased value claim, will enrich your body of beliefs and put you in better shape for taking part in discussions on that subject.

Perhaps it is fair to bring the methods together by remarking that brainstorming seems to be reflection with the aid of a pad and pencil, and that talking it out seems to be reflection with the help of one or more other persons. This is in keeping with the idea that each one of us must do his own thinking, must take responsibility for himself, in forming his body of value beliefs.

15

Spotting Camouflaged Value Judgments

In this chapter we examine two well-known and important documents, to detect value judgments embedded within them. I call these judgments "camouflaged" not because somebody was trying to conceal them, for value judgments weren't known as such when these writings were crafted, but because their value judgments blend in well with the factual background against which they are presented, and do not carry the usual flags or sign-words that make many value judgments easy to pick out. It is certain that neither Abraham Lincoln, in writing the address for Gettysburg, nor the framers of the Declaration of Independence had any thought about whether they were using value judgments (as formulated in this book) or not. But our study of both these documents shows that conceptions of *how things ought to be* functioned strongly in the minds of their authors.

AN EXCERPT FROM THE
DECLARATION OF INDEPENDENCE

When, in the course of human events, it becomes necessary for one people to dissolve the political bands which have connected them with another, and to assume among the powers of the earth, the separate and equal station to which the laws of nature and of nature's God entitle them, a decent respect to the opinions of mankind requires that they should declare the causes which impel them to the separation.

We hold these truths to be self-evident: That all men are created equal, that they are endowed by their Creator with certain unalienable rights, that among these are life, liberty, and the pursuit of happiness; that, to secure these rights, Governments are instituted among men, deriving their just powers from the consent of the governed; that, whenever any form of Government becomes destructive of these ends, it is the right of the people to alter or to abolish it, and to institute new Government, laying its foundation on such principles, and organizing its powers in such form, as to them shall seem most likely to effect their safety and happiness.

In examining the quoted passage to identify its value judgments, we start with the full sentences and main clauses. The first paragraph is in fact one full sentence, and its last clause is its main clause: "A decent respect to the opinions of mankind requires that they should declare the causes which impel them to the separation." This clause expresses the value assertion, "We *ought to* declare the causes that impel us to the separation" from Great Britain. The "decent respect" can only be a subjective notion, for it is not concrete in written law, hence the statement is not objectively testable. Moreover, "decent" is given the force of a value-expressing word, indicating that the respect that is mentioned is the kind that it ought to be, a respect toward mankind—persons, as value-judging agents forming "opinions" of the act of separation from the "people" or nation from which they are declaring themselves independent.

"We hold these truths to be self-evident . . ." is a fact-claiming proposition. The writers of the Declaration did actually hold the opinion that these statements were self-evidently true.

". . . that all men are created equal . . ." If this were received as an assertion of fact, it would be refuted by the facts that some men are stronger than others, some are more intelligent than others, some run faster, some hit baseballs farther, some woo more convincingly, and so on. The writers included this statement with the force of a value assertion: "All men *ought to be treated as though they were* created equal." This was the importance of it, and this was the idea that justified a long war for independence.

". . . that they are endowed by their Creator with certain unalienable rights. . . ." For the Founding Fathers this was a fact-claiming statement. They affirmed that it was the way things *are* that people had these rights.

". . . that among these are life, liberty, and the pursuit of happiness . . ." The source or the basis and guarantee of a right is something much under debate and discussion among social and political philosophers. For the time being, though, we may note that the writers of the Declaration are saying that "life is an unremovable right," "liberty is an unremovable right," "the pursuit of happiness is an unremovable right" that every person possesses. These, in turn, can be translated into their equivalent in our standard value language: "Every person ought to be regarded as having a right to life," "Every person ought to be regarded as having a right to liberty," and "Every person ought to be regarded as having a right to the pursuit of happiness." The justification for these claims has already been offered, namely, that the Creator has endowed us with these rights.

". . . whenever any form of Government becomes destructive of these ends, it is the right of the people to alter or abolish it, and to institute new Government . . ." This clause clearly states that when a government becomes destructive of its proper ends, *the people ought to be permitted* to alter it or abolish it and set up a new one.

Those are the value claims that are made at the level of main clauses in this portion of the Declaration of Independence. Other valuations made by the Founding Fathers are evident on a grammatically more subordinate level. Let us look at some of them.

"[When it becomes necessary] . . . to assume among the powers of the earth, the separate and equal station to which the laws of nature and nature's God entitle them . . ." These words do not make a full declaration that "*X* is a right" or "*X* ought to be the way it is," but they give rise to the inference that both natural and divine law provide that every "people" is entitled to a separate and equal station in the world with every other people. Interestingly, the Founding Fathers do not define what a "people" is, nor define the degree of impropriety by a government that makes revolution "necessary." The wording implies, "It is necessary *now*"; this inference is a factual proposition. The additional inference not directly stated, "every people ought to have a separate and equal station in the world," is a value judgment.

"Governments . . . deriving their just powers from the consent of the governed . . ." This ten-word modifier of "Governments" implies the value claim, "Governments derive their just powers from the consent of the governed," and strongly suggests the counterthesis (which is *not,* however, logically implied), "If governments derive their powers *without* the consent of the governed, these powers are not just." The word *just* in the sense of *fair* is what makes the statement a value claim. Just, fair, is how things ought to be.

". . . to institute new Government, laying its foundation on such principles, and organizing its powers in such form, as to them shall seem most likely to effect their safety and happiness." This says, "A government ought to be founded on such principles and in such a form as to ensure its people's safety and happiness, so far as they know how to bring about such a government."

Most discourses do not have such a heavy load of value claims as this passage. It is fitting, however, that in a declaration of independence many of these should appear, because after all, the people writing this document are setting out to attempt to create a government, and a nation, *as it ought to be!*

THE *GETTYSBURG ADDRESS* OF ABRAHAM LINCOLN
(NOVEMBER 19, 1863)

Fourscore and seven years ago our fathers brought forth upon this continent a new nation, conceived in liberty, and dedicated to the proposition that all men are created equal.

Now we are engaged in a great civil war, testing whether that nation, or any nation so conceived and so dedicated, can long endure.

We are met on a great battlefield of that war.

We have come to dedicate a portion of that field as a final resting place for those who here gave their lives that that nation might live.

It is altogether fitting and proper that we should do this.

But in a larger sense we cannot dedicate, we cannot consecrate, we cannot hallow this ground.

The brave men, living and dead, who struggled here, have consecrated it far above our poor power to add or detract.

The world will little note, nor long remember, what we say here, but it can never forget what they did here.

It is for us, the living, rather to be dedicated here to the unfinished work which they who fought here have thus far so nobly advanced.

It is rather for us to be here dedicated to the great task remaining before us, that from these honored dead we take increased devotion to that cause for which they gave the last full measure of devotion; that we here highly resolve that these dead shall not have died in vain, that this nation, under God, shall have a new birth of freedom, and that government of the people, by the people, and for the people, shall not perish from the earth.

The address begins with a fact-claiming statement: The United States was brought forth at the time and in the manner stated. The proposition that Lincoln gives in indirect quotation, you have already seen, is a value judgment ("All men are created equal"), but it occurs within a long modifier (the entire passage after *dedicated*) that is factual. That is, the nation *was* dedicated to this proposition. The Declaration of Independence is documentary evidence that this is the way it was. The next three statements ("Now we are engaged . . . ,We are met . . . ,We have come . . .") are also all fact-claiming.

With "It is altogether fitting and proper that we should do so," Lincoln gives us a value judgment. We are, he is saying, doing something that we ought to do.

The next two sentences are fact claims. They are subjective and interpretive, but nevertheless they are dealing with how things are, not with how things ought to be. The most important form of dedication, Lincoln is saying, has already taken place.

"The world will little note . . ." is fact-claiming, being predictive and testable by observation; "it can never forget . . ." is also fact-claiming. So far as the second claim is concerned, at least, Lincoln was right; the world has not forgotten what happened at Gettysburg.

"It is for us . . . to be here dedicated to the noble work . . ." is value-claiming. Lincoln is saying, "We ought to dedicate ourselves to the unfinished work of establishing this nation." The phrase "so nobly advanced" reflects Lincoln's admiring estimate of the soldiers' achievement and thus conveys a value judgment.

"It is rather for us . . ." is a phrase with which Lincoln again expresses "we ought," and gives greater specific meaning to his previous value claim. The phrase is used to introduce a series of value judgments. It supplies the "ought," and each subordinate clause beginning with *that* completes a separate value judgment. Since idiomatically we use *to* instead of *that,* following *ought,* I restate the value judgments thus: We ought to dedicate ourselves to the task of the soldiers' unfinished work; we ought to become increasingly devoted to their patriotic cause; we ought to highly resolve that they shall not have died in vain; we ought to highly resolve that the nation shall have a new birth of freedom; and we ought to highly resolve that this government, conceived and dedicated as already stated, shall not be destroyed.

Thus, besides containing one value assertion at about the midpoint, the speech ends with a series of six value-claiming propositions arranged in a long series, each one syntactically dependent on the phrase, "It is rather for us . . . ," which serves to express "We ought."

Before leaving this masterwork of oratory, we should acknowledge that there is a strong suffusion of value judging into the two sentences beginning "But in a larger sense . . ." and "The brave men. . . ." In these sentences, Lincoln compares two sets of people, those who fought and those who are present with him. He says that the sort of dedication, consecration, hallowing of the ground that was done by those who fought is far better, far more as such a thing ought to be, than the effort being made by those present with him at the time of the gathering at Gettysburg. This comes through not as a literal statement, but "between the lines," as an *implicit* value judgment.

We will see more examples of implicit value claims in chapter 17.

16

Levels of Value Claims

Near the beginning of this book I said that every sentence is either fact-claiming or value-claiming, and that the distinction between the two depends upon the main point of the sentence. In the material following, you have seen many examples typical of our use of language that bear out this statement. By now you have become adept at distinguishing between fact claims and value claims.

However, some writers, especially those with intricate or complex thoughts, mix factual and valuative ideas in a rich blend within a single sentence. We saw this to be true of the Declaration of Independence and the Gettysburg Address, which we examined in chapter 15. The sentences are still classifiable as one kind or the other, according to the main thought, but some communication of both sorts may be present. It is time now to see how to understand a sentence of that kind when we encounter one of them. Again, let us look at some simple examples:

1. Adam Smith's *Wealth of Nations,* while excelling other early works in economics, has little use as a textbook today.

    The main idea is factual: the book *The Wealth of Nations* is not much used as a textbook nowadays. The secondary idea is value-claiming: the book was excellent for its time. The speaker has mingled both the factual and the valuative mode in the same sentence. He places the value claim secondary to the factual claim by putting it in a subordinate grammatical structure. Perhaps the speaker gives the assertion "of little use" a semblance of valuation by contrasting it, using the word *while* (indicating "although") to do so, with the main value assertion; but still it is a testable fact.

2. Cora, whom he wed when he was twenty-seven, made him an admirable wife.

    This statement is value-claiming, surely. Cora was the kind of wife who was as a wife ought to be. The factual information of the man's age when married is expressed in a dependent clause, and is not the main idea of the statement.

3. I find it right that Shareholders International, a very sensible organization, stands up for stockholders' rights, which are very important to the stability of a free economy.

    This is value-claiming. The main clause, "I find it right . . ." surely conveys "is as it ought to be." There is another valuation in "a very sensible organization." The speaker or writer gives this one less emphasis by putting it in an appositional phrase rather than a clause like that constituting the main idea. That shareholders' rights are important to the stability of a free economy is a fact claim. Assertions that something is important, or of how important it is, are usually fact-claiming, because they usually are based on a measurable factor. To be important is not automatically to be good. The causes of a bad situation may include one that is more important than others; that does not mean that it is more as it ought to be than others.

(Notice that "I find it right" doesn't say the same sort of thing as "I think." The main clause doesn't merely say "here's what I am thinking." More strongly, it expresses that standing up for stockholders' rights is the right thing to do. The "finding" is figurative, not literal.)

Below is a more complex passage than those above. It is representative of the kind of prose that blends value judgments with factual assertions on both the primary level and the secondary level.

4. Ralph Nader, who in the past has performed nobly on behalf of consumers, was disaffected enough by NAFTA's [North American Free Trade Agreement] passage to try to make a class issue out of the trade treaty: He peddled the notion that if NAFTA is good for American business, it must be bad for working Americans.

   This is false. But the glib suggestion has worked its way into unfocused dialogue on radio and TV talk shows, and as the polls show, there are a lot of believers out there.[1]

   Let's start unpacking:

   The phrase ". . . who in the past has performed nobly on behalf of consumers . . ." is value-claiming. It says Nader did well. A secondary clause (a dependent clause, grammatically), it offers a value claim on the secondary level.

   "Ralph Nader . . . was disaffected by NAFTA's passage . . ." is fact-claiming. It says Nader didn't like NAFTA's passage.

   The infinitive construction ". . . to try to make a class issue out of the trade treaty . . ." is interpretative and an opinion, but it is fact-claiming. Either Nader tried, or he didn't try, to make NAFTA a class issue; whether he *ought* to have tried or whether it *ought* to be made a class issue is not stated. It is the author's opinion that disliking the trade treaty was what made Nader try to make it a class issue. That opinion is fact-claiming, whether or not it is true.

   "He peddled the notion that if NAFTA is good for American business it must be bad for working Americans." This is fact-claiming. There is some figurative language here, expressing that Nader tried to sell, or make acceptable ("peddled") the notion given, and since we tend to look down on peddling and peddlars, there is an unfavorable valuative suggestion in the choice of the word "peddled." Further, *notion* has suggestions of being vague, not carefully thought through, and unreliable. Again the author's language signals disapproval of Nader's response to NAFTA. However, the total effect of the sentence is *fact-claiming,* because the main thing said is that *Nader regarded* NAFTA as bad for American workers since it was good for American business. Either Nader did try to get this point across or he didn't. Whether he did could be determined in several ways—by reading Nader's writings, or by writing to him, or by calling him up and asking him. Notice how the author insinuates his disapproval *on a secondary level* by selecting words that have suggestions of unfavorable judgment. This technique is so easy and commonly practiced that probably all of us use it at times without even thinking about it.

You'll be glad to know that the author declares himself strongly in his next paragraph, and does not leave his disapproval merely on the level of insinuation. He says: "This is false. But the glib suggestion has worked its way into unfocused dialogue on radio and TV talk shows, and as the polls show, there are a lot of believers out there." This final sentence is fact-claiming, and the author himself gives us a way of testing it—polls that have been taken. You can appraise for yourself, by now, the choices of words and their effects that continue to show his disapproval.

But notice the most forceful words of all: "This is false." You and I know something about value-claiming propositions that the author either does not know or does not heed—that they don't have any true-false dimension. He would no doubt consider this a trivial, "academic" point, but our sounder conception of what value judgments can and cannot do should suggest to him a sounder outlook on the NAFTA controversy. Both value judgments, "NAFTA is good for American business" and "NAFTA is bad for working Americans," are wholly matters of opinion, not admitting of proof or disproof. One side's opinion is not automatically going to make the other side's opinion false.

What the author may legitimately say here, and probably what he would acknowledge that he intends to say, is that Nader's supposed contraries ("good for business, bad for workers") actually are not contraries at all, but rather that they are compatible with one another. In other words, a person may be wholly consistent in believing *both* that NAFTA will be good for American business *and* that it will be good for American workers.

NOTE

1. Hobart Rowen, "Capital Economics: The Job Ahead," *The Washington Post National Weekly Edition,* December 6–12, 1993, p. 5.

17

Implicit Value Claims

We now see that there are value claims presented in works of literature and other kinds of writing on at least three levels:

1. the main statement, expressed in an independent clause of its own;

2. the "secondary" or "subordinate" statement, expressed usually in a dependent clause, which is fairly important but not as important as the main statement; and

3. "fillers" that round out the thought with background rather than with the main or secondary-level assertions. They are usually expressed with value-laden words and phrases. (More of these will be shown in the next chapter.)

I suggest now that there is yet a fourth level. If you picture the levels as stacked one on top of the other, this one is at a "lower" level in the stack. It doesn't have specific sentences, clauses, or phrases as its vehicle. Rather, it has the whole communication—a paragraph, a letter, a chapter of a book, even a whole book. And while this makes such a claim far less obvious than the value claims given literally on the first three levels, it is sometimes the most important value claim of all.

We can call this the level of *implicit* value claims. In some cases it is obvious on the surface what the implicit claim of a passage is. In others a few moments' reflection is needed; in still others, the message may be heavily concealed and require careful thought to bring it out into the open. Writers whose main message is likely to get an adverse response will sometimes use implicit rather than direct statement to leave an idea with the reader, who remains to some degree unaware of it. Again, some writers will implant an important value claim at the implicit level but in an obvious way, because they regard that as the right way to give their point the proper amount of emphasis.

A single sentence may have an implicit but unstated value claim. Consider the following examples:

1. You *have* been paying your dues promptly *some of the time.* (Implicit value claim: You *ought to* pay your dues promptly *all of the time.*)

2. I'm sure you aren't going to wear that old torn and wrinkled jacket. (Implicit value claim: You ought not to wear that old torn and wrinkled jacket.)

3. Once he landed a job, Jack spent all of his weekly pay on clothes, dates, and drinks instead of putting away a portion of it as savings. (Implicit value claim: Jack should have put away a portion of his weekly pay as savings instead of spending it all on clothes, dates, and drinks.)

In the same way, a paragraph, even a whole essay, can convey a value claim without openly stating it. Here are two brief examples:

4. Elmer Ernst is running for Congress, and there are a few things he wants you to know. He is a family man who has been married twenty years and has two teenage daughters in public school. He has worked both for government and for private industry. He has been a member of the school board in his community for eight years, and a member of the city council of a city of 100,000 population for two terms. He has a strong interest in environmental affairs and educational matters. He has your interests at heart. And he has a wide reputation as a man you can trust. (Implicit value claim: You ought to vote for Elmer Ernst for Congress.)

5. The Knight in the triumph of his heart made several reflections on the greatness of the *British* Nation; as, that one *Englishman* could beat three *Frenchmen*; that we could never be in danger of Popery so long as we took care of our fleet; that the Thames was the noblest river in *Europe*; that *London Bridge* was a greater piece of work than any of the Seven Wonders of the World; with many other honest prejudices which naturally cleave to the heart of a true *Englishman*.

   —Joseph Addison, *Spectator* 383 (original italics) (Implicit value claim: The British nation is better, by far, than the French or any other.)

Even an entire book can convey a value claim implicitly. Even though I can't obviously reproduce a whole book here as an illustration, I will suggest a few examples that may be familiar to you.

Charles Dickens, *A Christmas Carol*: Everyone ought to give up the selfish viewpoint and conduct himself or herself with generous concern for others.

Harriett Beecher Stowe, *Uncle Tom's Cabin*: Slavery ought to be done away with.

Victor Hugo, *Les Misérables*: Our society and our justice system ought to be restructured so as to be fair to the common people.

George Orwell, *1984*: We ought to be aware that the kind of society described here is a possibility, and we ought to do everything we can to prevent it.

In recent times, the attitude has widely been taken toward books of fiction that they should not openly champion a cause, but should purely entertain. However, some of them do seem to press upon us what has lately been called "a hidden agenda." Moreover, there are many books of nonfiction whose statements are largely or entirely factual in nature, but that display, or betray, a "slant" or a valuation by the author of the main concept that he is treating. Besides these, there are many books of either fiction or nonfiction whose authors are attempting the expression of an *ought-*judgment. (An example is B. F. Skinner's *Walden II,* in which the author presents the implicit thesis, "A society ought to be ordered and conducted rationally.")

Therefore, it is a most useful tool for understanding a book, to ask the following questions:

1. Is there an underlying value assertion (or more than one) implicitly expressed in this book?

2. If so, what is it?

3. What is the fairest and most exact statement of it?

4. Ought I to believe it? Do I believe it already? Or do I believe something that is in conflict with it?

And from that point, let the discussion begin!

18

Value-Attributing Words and Phrases

Although most of our words are useful for imparting factual assertions, there are many words that mainly attribute value to something—that is, they mainly say that something is as it ought (or ought not) to be, rather than giving objective information about that thing. They enable a speaker or writer to give his subjective appraisal of it. These value-laden words and phrases range from the very broad to the very narrow. Some of them are praise-words that could be applied to almost anything, while others apply literally to something very specific and could not, except in a figurative way, apply to anything else.

For example, the word *neat* has been a slang expression for at least a century now, which we apply very broadly. Whether actual neatness or tidiness is involved or not, we use it to describe whatever we favor or regard to be as it ought to be—cars, girls, musical performances, games. On the other hand the word *ironclad* almost universally signifies favor, but it does not at all have such a wide range. It can be meaningfully applied only in connection with ships or similar structures (having its origin in the Civil War vessels *Monitor* and *Merrimac*), and in a figurative sense to such things as promises, guarantees, and contracts. To call a contract "ironclad," which is to say unbreakable, is to say that it is as it ought to be; thus *ironclad* conveys a value judgment. But it could not be applied sensibly to cars, girls, musical performances, or games with the freedom with which *neat* might be applied.

In this chapter we will observe examples of words that are used primarily to express a value judgment, and only incidentally, if at all, to impart factual information. Speakers and authors choose these words to attribute value of some kind to the objects, just as the words *green* and *purple* attribute color to the objects to which they are applied. But you have seen by now that value is not, like greenness and purpleness, a property of objects. Rather, it is a conception of what the object ought to be like, and an expression of value ordinarily states whether the object is or is not like what the speaker or writer believes it ought to be.

Consider the following group of examples:

1. This apple is delicious.
   This kidney pie is delicious.
   This honey is delicious.
   This chili con carne is delicious.

The propositions in the above list are expressed responses to taste, and they are all favorable to the food tasted. However, an apple does not taste like kidney pie, and honey does not taste like chili con carne. The only thing which the four mentioned foods have in common is that they have all been accorded the word *delicious*. Obviously, then, *delicious* does not mean having some common property of taste or flavor. Rather, it is a praise-word for all four foods, different though they are, and tells that, of its kind, *each is as it ought to be.*

2. Yummy, Mummy! This chocolate fudge is *good!*

In a context of things to eat, the word *good* is indeed a value-expressing word. It is probably limited in its meaning to the idea *delicious,* or good-tasting. To employ either term in describing a food is a valuation, and yields a value-claiming proposition.

3. In her youth she was beautiful.

The chief idea of the statement is contained in the word *beautiful.* What *beautiful* conveys here is that appearance is being spoken about, and that with respect to it she was as she ought to be. No factual information is given; we don't know whether "she" was tall, short, or average, light- or dark-haired, blue- or brown-eyed, and so on. Therefore, this example is a value-claiming proposition.

4. He waved to the beautiful girl who was coming across the footbridge.

In the third example, *beautiful* concluded a main clause, so as a value-laden word it made the main idea a value claim. But in this example it has the lesser status of an adjective modifying *girl,* the object of a preposition, while the main thought, the factual claim "he waved . . . ," is also the main clause. Thus *beautiful* here is placed, by the choice of its degree of grammatical subordination, in a position of subordinate emphasis. The total effect of the example is fact-claiming; yet the writer manages to get in one value claim along with the facts that he relays to us.

5. The writing in these books is great writing.

Greatness is a quality often sought in writing; especially in the writing of books. However, the word *great* imparts to us only the idea that someone evaluates the writing in the mentioned books as extremely high, without informing us of any of its specific characteristics, or of what constitutes great writing. This, too, is a value-claiming proposition.

6. A relief pitcher, Morgan is always cool-headed under pressure.

The meaning of *cool-headed* here can be more or less completely specified in objective terms, describing Morgan's behavior: he takes his time getting ready to pitch, he watches the catcher's signal closely, he considers how many runners are on base, he reminds himself where to throw the ball if it is batted to him, and so on. However, our culture and traditions have made cool-headedness a virtue, and *cool-headed* a value term.

To the extent that the sentence might be intended to describe Morgan's behavior, it is fact-claiming. But, the word being what it is in our culture, the sentence is probably intended to bestow *cool-headed* on Morgan as a compliment. That makes the statement value-claiming, and, therefore, probably intended more to let us know about Morgan's way of thinking and acting than about his actual behavior. Morgan, it is saying, is in this respect as a relief pitcher ought to be. To be sure, we have to read statements like this in context and carefully consider from the *evidence of the context* what the author is trying to do. Having done so, we find that there is at least an implicit, or indirect, value judgment here.

7. Her knowledge of music was nothing to write home about.

The phrase *nothing to write home about* is idiomatic, if not slang, for a low valuational rating. It signals that its subject is very little as she ought to be, with respect to knowledge of music. No additional factual information is added to the sentence by these words. The sentence is value-claiming in its main meaning.

8. Both his face and his manners were ugly.

This sentence with its "both . . . and . . ." pattern manages to speak about two things at the same time. It states strongly that neither is as it ought to be, and is clearly value-claiming in both its main ideas.

9. The weather in New Orleans is ideal at this time of year.

The word *ideal* is widely used to mean "perfect, as good as it can be," although it has a historically prior meaning, "relating to ideas." In both its adjectival form and noun form (as in, "In finally winning the Tutwiler Prize, he reached his ideal"), it is commonly a value-attributing word, and the statement is value-claiming.

10. He is a careful driver.

Contrast this statement with "He is a cautious driver." We tend to use *careful* of drivers when the most important thing we mean is *cautious,* that is, having a habit of guarding against collision and other dangers. Yet a driver who is careful may perform other actions of driving carefully without performing them cautiously, such as shifting gears without grinding them, aiming the rearview mirror so that it includes the entire rear window, and fastening his seat belt upon entering the vehicle. Both of these words say, "In respect to being a driver, he is as he ought to be." One of them (*careful*) covers more territory than the other (*cautious*). Moreover, *cautious* could be specified rather objectively, as we did above with *cool-headed*; thus it could convey some objective information as well as give a valuation.

11. His ability to absorb and remember tiny details is amazing.

Would this sentence convey *ought-to-be,* in every context? We normally use *amazing* as a value-assigning word. However, in a context where the question was raised whether people actually were amazed or not, it could be fact-claiming.

Being amazed is a psychological condition. We probably experience it rather rarely, but knowing of it suggests to us that we can express that certain things are as they ought to be by the exaggerated expression, "That's amazing." Judgments on the question of fact or value claim should always be made in connection with the context, when it is available.

12. Junior! Now you are being obnoxious!

Here is a value-attributing word that attributes a low, indeed a very low, value to Junior—to his present behavior, at any rate.

13. The unfair action taken by the hearing officer meant that Josh had no opportunity to find a decent job.

By using the word *unfair,* the speaker clearly regards the hearing officer's action as one that ought not to be undertaken. This is a moral value claim on a lower level of importance in a fact-claiming (even if opinionated) statement.

14. Regrettably, George continued to scold the child long after her remorseful tears were dry.

The word *regrettably,* starting off this sentence and applying to its whole idea, is a value-judgmental word. It assumes someone's viewpoint—that of the speaker, that of an outside observer, possibly even that of George himself—and indicates "not as it ought to be" from that viewpoint. The rest of the sentence is quite factual, but the strongest idea is that of George's continued scolding being improper. "Regrettably" in this sentence connotes "George ought not to have scolded the child any more."

15. Chad had found the perfect place for an artist to have a vacation.

A fact is asserted here, namely, that Chad had found someplace for a vacation, but the main idea is in the word *perfect,* which clearly states that the place is absolutely as it ought to be for vacationing. Hence the statement is value-claiming.

16. Seasoned Bridge Player: "Why, this hand's a Yarborough!"
    Novice Bridge Player: "What's a Yarborough?"
    S.B.P.: "It's a hand like this! There's not a face card nor an ace in it!"

Sometimes we express our value judgments by using language that puts the evaluated thing in a category, as the seasoned bridge player here has done. The word that names the category is what makes the assertion a value judgment. Other examples are *junk, trash,* or, on the favorable side, *a sweetheart, the cat's pajamas, a dream.*

The above are only a very few of the many words and phrases, favorable or adverse, that attribute value to their object. It would be impossible to catalog all of them. However, we can confidently follow the grammarian's and linguistic analyst's advice to identify the *function* of the word. Does it impart objective information to the discourse as its chief function? Then it is not a value-attributing word. Does it serve the chief purpose of indicating "ought to be" (or "ought not to be")? Then it is a value-attributing word, and if it is on the main rather than a lower level in the sentence, it makes the sentence a value claim. On a lower level, it strongly suggests a value claim that is not fully stated.

In the examples given we see words—*excelling, admirable, sensible*—that have as their principal job the expressing of a valuation, while along with that they may give or suggest some factual detail. Adjectives like these can be tucked into statements that have as their main job the assertion of something factual. These are called *value-laden* words. Some typical examples follow:

Favorable Value-Laden Words	Adverse Value-Laden Words
Delicious	Foul-tasting
Fair	Unfair
Beautiful	Ugly
Praiseworthy	Blameworthy
Popular	Unpopular
Likeable	Repulsive
Excellent	Poor
Neat	Dirty
Fruitful	Fruitless

Favorable Value-Laden Words	Adverse Value-Laden Words
Fascinating	Boring
Smart	Dumb
Wise	Unwise
Welcome	Unwelcome
Superior	Inferior
Well-rounded	Mediocre
Stunning	Dowdy
Well-dressed	Ill-dressed
Crackerjack	Ineffectual
Courteous	Uncouth
Keen	Dull
Leading	Backward
Peachy	Rocky
Giant	Monster
Wholesome	Unwholesome
Wonderful	Terrible

There are hundreds more. There are words having what many rhetoricians have called "favorable connotations" or "unfavorable connotations." However, some of them are so purely valuative that their meanings are virtually *nothing but* connotation, lending little or no factual detail to a statement.

In its richness and expressiveness, the English language does not confine words such as those above to a single function. There are times when we encounter one of them with a somewhat different meaning, or even a quite different meaning, so we cannot say simply, "Watch for these words, and when you find one of them you have a value judgment." In this as in all contexts the test of whether a word, a phrase, or a clause is used to express a value judgment is whether what it fundamentally says is, "is as it ought to be," or "happened as it ought to happen."

19

Defining and Quantifying the Good

"How good does something have to be, to be called 'good'?"

In nearly all areas of human work or recreation, there are things that must be of a certain quality in order to fulfill the purposes of those activities. Quite often, in those pursuits agreed standards arise of what is good, what is not so good, and what is bad. Over time, these standards tend to become commonly understood definitions, or specifications, of what may be called "good." And, of course, when a practitioner of one of these pursuits calls something "good" he is clearly affirming that it is as it ought to be. Thus, when these standards are applied, they act as ready-made judgments on the worth or value of the things involved, so that time is saved that otherwise would be spent pondering decisions on values. Further, through these standards persons new to the field of activity concerned benefit from the experience of previous value judges.

Let's study some details in the following:

1. These tires are still good. They have been on the road only four thousand miles.

It is usual for motorists to judge tires by one principal property, the ability to give service on the road. Thus the way these tires ought to be is to have the ability to give further service. "Good" in this context is defined, informally, in that single respect. These "good" tires can still give many more miles of service on the road.

2. This light bulb is still good. Put it up on the shelf with the new ones.

In this case also, "good" means only one thing. With light bulbs, it is the ability to give light when electricity is passed through them. *Good* here has the very narrow definition, "capable of giving light when switched on." But these first two examples can both be understood in a broader sense, namely, "capable of serving the purpose for which it was intended." This can apply equally well to tires and light bulbs, and many other objects: spark plugs, paper towels, artificial eyelashes, playing cards, glass jars, computer chips, or disposable cigarette lighters.

3. This offer is good only until November 30. (Said by a potential buyer of a house to its seller.)

This one is a little complex and a bit ambiguous. We can think of various offers, say, of money to be paid for a house that is on the market. We generally think that there are good offers and others that aren't so good, maybe actually bad. A good offer, one that is as it ought to be from the point of view of the seller, is one that is the most like the amount of money he wants to be paid for his house.

But obviously that isn't the meaning that the bidder has in mind in making statement 3. Naturally, he will claim that the amount of money he mentions is "a good offer" for the seller in the sense just described, and he and the seller may even agree on that. But the bidder's meaning is that after the stated date, the offer is not "good" because it is canceled—it isn't even an offer any more! So here *good* has taken on a new meaning. The life of the offer has been given a limit, that number of days until November 30, at the end of which it is no longer viable, but instead dead or nonexistent.

4. The patient's temperature is two degrees above normal. We've got to bring it down.

What is to be noted here is that *normal* is equated with the good, what the patient's temperature *ought to be.* In many settings, the normal (the usual, the "average") is taken for "as it ought to be." This equivalency should not be applied haphazardly, how-ever, for in many situations what happens most often is decidedly not what most persons would say ought to be. If most Ethiopian children have bloated bellies because of a starvation diet, should we say that *all* Ethiopian children ought to have bloated bellies, since that is "normal"?

5. In our grading system, A is excellent, B is good, C is average, D is below average, and E is failing.

Here a five-term vocabulary is worked out, and is declared in advance of the value judging that is expected to take place. The terms are the first five letters of the English alphabet. Two of them, *excellent* and *good,* are so defined as to indicate favorable quality, *below average* and *failing* connote unfavorable quality, and *average* indicates "neither." All the terms have become valu-ative words for this use, and when employed as predicates they yield value-claiming judgments.

Notice that while *average* has a popular meaning of "usual," "ordinary," it also has a mathematical meaning that is perhaps equally prominent. In neither meaning does it necessarily serve as a value-assigning term, although occasionally people interpret it that way; some consider it a compliment to be called average, while others regard it as a derogatory judgment. *Failing* has no mathematical meaning, but has a strong evaluative meaning in everyday usage.

The mention of mathematical meaning leads us very naturally to the subject of special meanings for value terms that constitute mathematically interpreted standards. Let's explore this concept with some more examples.

6. This afternoon, the air is at the ideal temperature.

What is the ideal temperature? There is a tradition that it is 72 degrees Fahrenheit. That's thought to be neither too hot nor too cold. But who's making the judgment? Perhaps a weather expert or some group of them, or perhaps just ordinary people who know when they feel comfortable. It was someone's judgment, at some time and place, that gave the tradition its start. The word *ideal* surely means "as it ought to be," and this is an example of the assignment of a mathematical quantity to it, to be its meaning in a special context. The value judging has already been made in the past, so that when you discover the temperature to be 72 degrees Fahrenheit, you can call it ideal without fear of dispute. Unlike the first five examples, this one not only has a special narrow meaning but expresses that special meaning in terms of a quantity.

7. Although he was handicapped and confined to a wheel chair, he had 20-20 vision.

The rating of 20-20 for vision is usually taken to represent the perfect; it is considered that nobody has any better vision than 20-20. This betokens the ability clearly to distinguish letters subtending twenty seconds of arc at a distance of twenty feet. To go up or down on the figures before or after the hyphen would indicate farsightedness, nearsightedness, or another impairment. Thus this formula is a specification of the way vision ought to be.

8. He was legally intoxicated, too drunk to drive, having an alcohol content in the blood of 0.08 percent.

Most states have a legislatively established definition of what constitutes intoxication to the extent that the subject is a hazard if he or she drives. In Florida in 1993, a person was legally too intoxicated to drive if his or her blood contained 0.10 percent of alcohol by volume. An act of the legislature made the standard, as of 1994, more strict, 0.08 percent instead of 0.10 percent. Thus some people who were formerly sober were made drunk by definition!

9. Says a weather broadcaster: "The small particle count this afternoon is 27, in the 'good' range."

Meteorologists have established that the "good range" of air quality is one in which there are between one and fifty parts per million of undesirable gases or solid substances in our atmosphere. This has become the standard of the Environmental Protection Agency. Next comes the "moderate" range, of 51 to 100 parts per million; 101 to 199 is "unhealthful"; 200 to 299 is "very unhealthful"; and 300 and above is "hazardous." It is usual to accept a "good range" as "the range within which it ought to be." Thus we have professional judgment setting the pace for us in adjudging whether our air is sufficiently pure. Most of us would be willing to leave judgment in the matter to these experts, because we believe that they have better means than we do to determine where the margin is, beyond which impurities in the air begin to become harmful.

In this vocabulary, the term used at one end, *good,* is clearly purely valuative, and "The count is in the good range" is a value claim, meaning, "So far as small particles of matter in the air are concerned, the air is good." At the other end, however, the term *hazardous* is specifiable in concrete experience. It is not a valuative term in itself, but is a value-laden factual term; it conveys that in the air so described, persons with asthma are very likely to suffer attacks, while persons whose breathing is normal run the risk of having swelling and inflammation of their airways, and so on. These effects can be observed physically.

So how good does something have to be, to be called "good"? Often, it has to be within a certain range on a scale. When the need for standards of comparison is great, responsible authorities or the general public find ways to assign "values"—specific figures of measurement—according to a scale within whose ranges individual cases can be assigned. The value-judging function is not set aside or canceled. Rather, it is performed in advance for a great many cases. Past experience has shown what measurements lie "in the good range," or are "admissible" or "acceptable" or "ideal." It becomes easier to express how good individual cases are when a scale has been devised or a framework of terms set up on which they may be graded. The scale, of course, is not a part or a property of the material being rated, but is imposed upon that material by persons who are seeking precise ways in which to express their value judgments.

20

Are They Value Claims or Not? Ambiguous Sentences

Sentences can be ambiguous—that is, they can mean either of two things. Take the following example:

Captain, the boat is fast.

The sailor's report can mean either that the boat moves swiftly, or that it is moored and therefore not moving at all.

Here are some ambiguous newspaper headlines, whose writers didn't realize the possible second meaning:

Hopis hoping to see D.C. close up.

Was that about a bus tour of Washington, or about what the Hopis think the government deserves?

Credit life expensive, unnecessary group says.

From the point of view of life insurance companies, the group probably *is* unnecessary. But from the point of view of the group, it's the credit insurance that is unnecessary.

Value claims are no exception. They can be ambiguous, too. But the interesting, and problem-creating, thing about them is that some statements are ambiguous by being value-claiming under one interpretation, and fact-claiming under the other. Let's examine some examples.

1. Hackhorn has gone the farthest of any of our employees in striving for excellence.

If there is some sort of objective measurement, such as the number of postgraduate courses taken, showing how far Hackhorn has gone in comparison with other employees, then this can be an assertion of a verifiable fact. But if there is no such measure, the statement expresses a subjective opinion and is valuative, saying that Hackhorn has been the most like what an employee ought to be in seeking excellence (whatever excellence is!).

2. He's my first choice.

One must consult context to interpret this one. It is factual, of course, that "he" *is* my first choice, meaning that I have chosen him first. Thus far, it is a fact-claiming statement. However, the force of this sentence might be "He in my opinion is the best," or ". . . the best suited," or the like. If we didn't have something like that to say also, then "He's my first choice" probably wouldn't get said. On the other hand, if the *chief* purpose of the statement is to affirm that "he" is the best of available choices, then the statement functions as a value judgment. It is completely possible that it actually works, in its social as well as verbal context, to convey both fact and value judgments.

Again, the sentence is ambiguous in this regard: It can mean "I had the opportunity to make several choices, and he was the one I chose first," as, for example, in the annual draft of professional baseball players; or it can mean "I chose him *to be* first," as, for instance, when I had a job opening to fill, I chose him as the first one to whom to offer the job, while having in mind which applicant I'd offer it to second, if he declined. With either interpretation—that is, with either intention on the part of the speaker—the same ambiguity identified previously, as to whether it is a fact or value judgment, remains.

3. My desktop is an untidy mess.

This sounds like a value-claiming proposition. It certainly is saying, "My desktop is not as it ought to be," and in that way it is expressing a value judgment. However, there are some pretty widely agreed-upon standards about what constitutes a tidy or an untidy desktop. That means that the meaning of the phrase "untidy mess" is ambiguous. One of its meanings is factual, and the other is valuative. So far as the meaning is factual, it is provable, and that is a sure sign that the statement is a statement about the actual world that exists. An absolutely clear desktop, one with not a single object upon it, would be a tidy desktop, by the general understanding of what "tidy" means, and we can look at the desktop to see whether it is clear. To that extent, the word *tidy* is factual and measurable. To go further: Suppose the desktop contains papers stacked in a basket in one corner, and a row of pencils and ball-point pens arranged along the opposite side. Still tidy, no? Not untidy at all. But now add more and more papers, all at odd angles to one another all over the surface, a half-full ashtray with a few cigarette butts resting outside of it, a spilled tray of paper clips, two open books, an appointment pad opened to a date two weeks ago, an empty stapler, a heavy pair of scissors being used as a paperweight to hold a checkbook open, and a leather bag for holding no one knows what. Maybe a few employees, but no supervisors, would call *that* a tidy desktop. If that's the way my desk looks, then "My desktop is an untidy mess" is verifiable as true, therefore fact-claiming, in the widely understood concept of a tidy desk, or an untidy one.

But suppose that my desk has four or five objects, or a dozen, that are partly organized and partly in disarray, and then I say, "My desktop is an untidy mess." As far as the understood factual concepts are concerned, it's in a gray area. But in my own judgment, it ought to be more tidy than it is. Thus my remark that it is an untidy mess is a value claim.

4. George weighs too much.

Without the context, we're a little at sea with this one. Does George weigh too much to fly in an ultralight aircraft? Too much to wear Dad's hand-me-down overalls? Or too much according to height-and-weight norms used by doctors' offices and insurance companies?

In connection with that last possibility, one could say quite objectively, perhaps while looking at one of the tables of heights and weights, "George weighs too much." This might be news to George. It could, in other words, have the force simply of a fact-claiming statement, taking the table of weights and heights as establishing what objectively is too much. On the other hand, someone could be using the expression to tell George that his weight is not as it ought to be, that he should change it by reducing. In a case like this one, context is everything, and we need more information from context in order to understand fully what we have been told.

5. Headline: Critics contend cats should breed in wild.

This headline was about Florida panthers and Texas cougars, and man's efforts to replenish their species. Did it mean that the wildcats *ought to* be left to breed in the wild, to prevent their dying out, rather than being brought into a zoo to be bred? Or did it mean that if they were left in the wild, it was reasonable to infer that they would indeed breed and multiply? Upon reading the news story, I discovered that some people wanted to breed the cats under controlled conditions, but their critics believed *both* meanings of the above ambiguous headline; that is, that the cats *ought* to be left to breed in the wild, and that they *would.*

Language is a slippery thing after all, isn't it?

21

Expressing Values in Words

Recently I read that Senator Thomas A. Daschle of South Dakota, as Senate Minority Leader, was taking renewed interest in defining his party in terms of "government policies that reflect the values of working families."[1] I should have liked to ask Senator Daschle what values he meant by "the values of working families," and I strongly suspect that he would have spoken of them by name—that is, by words and phrases that name them. That has been the usual way of identifying values in our culture. But you will have noticed by now that as a specific way of expressing what we think constitutes a given value, it is far inferior to the value-claiming proposition.

In this chapter we will look at some of the many ways of expressing certain familiar values in propositions, in order to represent them more exactly in our thinking. Our specific results here are important, but the methods illustrated for finding expressions for our own and others' values are still more important.

We will now be looking at values that are introduced simply by their names—words or phrases—rather than already formulated in complete-sentence value judgments. Most of the campaign rhetoric and the reformers' speeches present values merely by their names, such as "honesty," "integrity," "cooperativeness," "American values," "family values," "the good life," "the American dream," "economic security," "a sound education," and "a better life for our children." Our present project is to progress from the names of our own or others' values to fully stated value judgments connoted by them that are capable of being believed or disbelieved.

It is essential to our endeavor to recognize that given terms, including the names of values, do not uniformly mean the same thing to everyone, but may mean different things to different people. Since values have no counterparts in the material world, we may expect this to be true of all or nearly all of them. Therefore, a highly necessary skill in the wording of values is conceiving of and recording different possible meanings that various people may assign to these terms. After we do that, we should attempt in each case to decide which, among the various potential meanings, is probably that intended by the speaker or writer whose thoughts we are examining.

THE CASE OF THE FOUNDING FATHERS

The Declaration of Independence states that "all men are created equal, that they are endowed by their Creator with certain unalienable rights, that among these are life, liberty, and the pursuit of happiness." Since these last three terms express the justification for government which motivated our forefathers to establish a government of their own, many persons regard "life, liberty, and the pursuit of happiness" as the primary "American values." On the whole, both Americans and non-Americans seem to accept the statement that these are unalienable. Yet, since the document does not state exactly what they are, they are still subject to interpretation.

Let's think about each in turn. Here are some tentative interpretations of those values known as *life, liberty,* and *the pursuit of happiness* that were listed in the Declaration:

1. Life

It is good to be alive, and a nation ought to provide the conditions under which each individual can maintain life as long as possible, his person being kept safe and secure from danger.

2. Liberty

Every individual ought to have the utmost of freedom consistent with public safety and with justice toward all, and a nation ought to provide the conditions under which such freedom is possible for each individual.

3. The Pursuit of Happiness

Every person has a right to pursue his own happiness, regardless of what form he considers it to take, to the extent that his efforts are consistent with public safety and respectful of the rights of others; and the nation ought to maintain the conditions under which each individual can carry on his search for happiness.

I believe that items 1, 2, and 3 express fair interpretations of what the Founding Fathers probably had in mind when they wrote the Declaration. However, many other interpretations are also possible, and in attempting to interpret the Founders' full intentions, it is good to be aware of a number of them. Let us look at the three terms again.

Do you consider that no. 1 affirms that there ought to be no abortions?

Do you consider that it prohibits capital punishment?

Do you consider that the quotation from the Declaration of Independence given above shows that the Founding Fathers intended to outlaw abortion and capital punishment?

I think it would be reasonable to say that the Founding Fathers did not have abortion in mind, since there was general social agreement against abortion in their time. Neither, I think, did they have capital punishment in mind, since their morality, founded on the religion of the time, permitted capital punishment. However, someone *nowadays* stating that life is an American value might intend that his remark would treat abortion or capital punishment as wrong, a violation of an unalienable right.

For a moment, set aside your own belief on abortion, if you have one. Can you restate the first interpretation, "Life," as an *ought*-statement to make it show plainly that abortion would be considered wrong? And then can you restate the same proposition in an *ought*-statement that would permit abortion?

When you have completed these two tasks, you will have shown yourself that you are able to see both sides of a controversial question, not just the side that you happened to start out with. And you will probably also have revealed to yourself that the problem even of stating the abortion issue, much less taking sides on it, is deeper and more complex than you had previously realized.

Here are some possible ways of answering these questions:

1a. Permitting abortion

It is good to be alive, and a nation ought to provide the conditions under which each individual born can maintain life as long as possible, being kept safe and secure from danger.

1b. Prohibiting abortion

It is good to be alive, and a nation ought to provide the conditions under which each person, including potential persons such as human embryos and foetuses, can maintain life as long as possible, being kept safe and secure from danger.

The instance of abortion in relation to life as a right helps show that some terms seem equally to include or to exclude certain crucial interpretations, and suggests why the courts must look deep under the surface to determine the apparent intentions of the writers of documents such as the Constitution, which is crucial to interpretation of our laws. We are far better off if we become alert to the possibilities of these differing interpretations than if we rest on our own unexamined assumptions about the intentions of those writers as to what their names of values actually mean.

THE CASE OF THE PRESIDENT'S HARD WORK

In his 1993 inaugural speech President Bill Clinton referred to the value of *hard work*. To call hard work a value is to say that there is something about it that is as it ought to be. But by referring to it while not describing it more exactly, President Clinton keeps us from knowing exactly what he means. Which of the following—if any—do you believe is his real meaning?

2a. The work we do ought to be difficult.

2b. Americans all ought to get jobs that are difficult work, rather than easy work.

2c. Some Americans, but probably not all of them, ought to get jobs that are difficult work rather than easy work.

2d. Americans ought to be willing, for the good of the country, to do work that is difficult.

2e. Americans ought to be glad that some other Americans are willing to do work that is difficult.

2f. Americans ought to believe that they can realize the "American Dream" for themselves by putting out great effort to reach it.

2g. America can be a great and wonderful nation if its people will put out great effort for their country.

2h. Americans ought to believe that by putting out plenty of effort they can help make and keep America a great and wonderful nation, they ought to resolve to do it, and they ought to do it.

Or do you think that President Clinton meant any and all of these, and would be happy to have his listeners accept one of them at random while ignoring the others?

It would have helped us know the president's precise meaning if he had followed the remark listing hard work as a value with a statement something like this: "We all ought to believe that America can be a great and wonderful nation for all its citizens, and we all ought to work hard, continually exerting our best efforts to make it so."

THE CASE OF "AMERICAN VALUES"

In reading my daily newspaper I have seen that various individuals—school board members, clergy, teachers, parents, and ordinary citizens—agree that the homes, churches, and schools ought to "teach our young people some values."

The theme they agree on pretty plainly assumes that our schools, churches, and families at present do *not* teach the young people any values. On the contrary, I am sure that sociologists, psychologists, experts on education, and others would say that part of the problem is that our schools, families, even churches are teaching values all right, but often teaching the societally *wrong* values.

It has been argued that society teaches young criminals wrong values by sending them to prison, where they meet expert burglars, lock pickers, car thieves, and similarly skilled felons. There, they learn the value that is expressed in the saying, "If a thing is worth doing at all, it is worth doing well." Accordingly they learn to be expert burglars, expert lock pickers, and expert car thieves. Thus, although they have learned one "right" value, they have learned many "wrong" values through this experience.

But back to school. I hope that the writers and speakers who want the schools and other institutions to "teach our young people some values" agree in general on *which* values the young people should be taught. I also hope that the values agreed upon are in some sense the "right" values, aside from the mere fact that they are the most popular. It is probably too much to hope that the values our young people are taught in their formative years will comprise a systematic, self-consistent value system. There is probably not enough agreement within our diverse society to determine just what that system ought to be.

Although it would be desirable to have one, let us not try to set out here a broad value system that is perfectly consistent within it-self and that would gain the approval of every individual. Rather, let's look at some of the values that people have suggested in their speeches, letters to the editor, and other public expressions as those that should be taught to the young:

Patriotism
Democracy
Good Citizenship
Clean Living
Sportsmanship
Fair Play
Law and Order
Family
God
Church
Education
Private Property
Self-Development
Service to Others
Health and Fitness
Human Rights

A list like this provides much exercise, for those who believe in intellectual rigor, in stating values. For example, what is it about patriotism that constitutes it as a value? If I were to try to show that patriotism is a value, I would probably say that what the term means to me is that "I ought to respect and support my na-tion as strongly as possible, accepting and attempting to improve its weaknesses while recognizing and working so as to maintain its strengths and to keep it a fitting object of everyone's admira-tion and affection."

Will you indulge me by letting me try a similar expression for family? "I ought to behave in a loving way toward the members of my immediate and my extended family, recognizing both their individuality and their kinship with the others, and I ought to try to perceive as underlying it all that which is the family as an institution in a society, so as to give the family in society full credit for all that it contributes to that society."

Do you see what the possibilities are? By admitting a word or phrase to a list of values, we give ourselves the opportunity to explore and express exactly what we mean by it. The important point here is not that you, my reader, should become persuaded that it is exactly what I have said about patriotism or the family, and nothing else, that makes them values. Rather, the point is the enrichment of our understanding that occurs when we transform the mere word or phrase into a fully and carefully stated value judgment that expresses what we believe or helps us to arrive at a belief in place of a vacancy in our belief structure.

THE CASE OF "FAMILY VALUES"

What do people mean when they say "family values"? This is one of the vaguest of all phrases relating to value. The following are some judgments that many would call to mind upon hearing the phrase "family values." As you read them, ask yourself whether all of them are necessary to the meaning of the phrase "family values." Are most of them? Are *any* of them?

Married couples ought to have children.

A child ought to grow up in a family, with both parents present.

Every child ought to have at least one brother or sister, unless there are extremely important reasons against it.

A loving child, upon attaining maturity, ought to marry and give his or her parents grandchildren.

Even single persons or couples without children ought to believe in the worth of family values.

The members of a family ought to eat dinner together in their own home every day.

The members of a family ought to participate in recreational activities together regularly, at least once a week.

The members of a family ought to go together to their place of worship regularly.

The members of a family ought to discuss together public matters that will have an impact upon them as a family.

The members of a family ought to have the habit of helping one another.

Family members ought to help one another in ways beyond what they would normally do for persons outside the family.

Every family member always ought to side with any family member who is engaged in a dispute with someone outside the family.

It is good for the children of a family to receive more education than was possible for their parents.

It is good for the parents of a family to provide advantages for their children that they themselves never had.

It is good for the elders in a family to let those of the younger generation know how tough life can be, so the younger members will not take for granted things that the elders obtained only through great striving and effort.

All of the above judgments clearly relate to family values, and many are important in the belief structures of those who declare that they champion family values. Yet no single one of the above expressions, and no specific group of them taken together, is able to state fully the entire meaning of the phrase *family values.* When that is the case, isn't it true that the phrase "family values" is indeed *very* vague? There is no single thing that it means, and no clear choice of alternatives of what it might mean. And when that is so, has a politician, a clergyman, a school board member, or anyone said much of anything when he or she has stated that we need a return to "family values"?

It would be more meaningful, hence more helpful, for such a speaker to single out one or just a few of the possible value judgments that he has in mind when referring to "family values," and to explain just why he selects that one and how he justifies his claim, to try to make us believe it. The clergyman, for example, could say, "Of the family values that I find important, I especially believe that it is good for the members of a family to attend church together, because . . ." Or the politician might say, "Of the family values that I find important, I especially believe that it is good for family members to discuss together public affairs that will have an impact upon them as a family, because . . ." In that fashion, the speaker will encourage further thinking about the claims he makes in the name of family values, rather than using vagueness to put an end to thinking.

NOTE

1. *Washington Post National Weekly Edition,* February 27–March 5, 1995, p. 14.

22

How Valid Arguments Work

This chapter gives a semester's deductive logic course in five minutes, but doesn't stop there. It goes on to show something about the logic of value-claiming propositions, a topic the usual one-semester logic course never mentions.

There are two main forms of deductive argument that we use daily. These forms or patterns of arguments are open to various fallacies, but here we shall speak only of the valid ones. What's "valid"? If the premises of an argument are true, and the argument is constructed in the right way, then the conclusion has to be true; it can be no other way. That's what *valid* means in logic.

The first form of argument deals with individual units and with groupings of units called *classes*:

A. All a are b.
    All b are c.
    Therefore, all a are c.

The letters *a, b,* and *c* stand for classes of things. They could be gym shoes, athletic shoes, and (simply) shoes, for example. Or they could be citizens of Lagos, Nigerians, and Africans. Those are examples of classes.

Variations on this pattern include:

B. All a are b.
   Smith is a.
   Therefore, Smith is b.

Smith is in a class by himself! For logic purposes, a single individual is considered a class. The a and b could be salaried workers and employees, for example, or shortstops and infielders, or whatnot.

The second main form of deductive argument deals with whole sentences or *propositions,* and uses the concepts *if* and *then* to yield conclusions.

C. If proposition P is true, then proposition Q is true.
   If proposition Q is true, then proposition R is true.
   Therefore, if proposition P is true, then proposition R is true.

And a variation:

D. If proposition P is true, then proposition Q is true.
   Proposition P *is* true.
   Therefore, Proposition Q *is* true.

There is a lot more to it than what's given here, but the main point is that for an argument to yield any truth, it has to have something true in it to start with, and then has to be constructed in the right way.

Here are some concrete examples that follow the given patterns.

A'. All "Boll Weevils" are Southern senators.
    All Southern senators are occasional residents of Washington.
    Therefore, all "Boll Weevils" are occasional residents of Washington.

B'. All Mohawks are Native Americans.
Alice Hogan is a Mohawk.
Therefore, Alice Hogan is a Native American.

C'. If a person has been elected to the Senate, then he or she has advertised widely in the public news media.
If a person has advertised widely in the public news media, then he or she has spent vast sums of money.
Therefore, if a person has been elected to the Senate, then he or she has spent vast sums of money.

D'. If dogs can swim, then they do not fear water.
Dogs can swim.
Therefore, dogs do not fear water.

If you will study the above four patterns, and the examples in which the single letters, *a, b, c,* in each pattern are assigned meanings in words, you will see that, provided you stick to the same meanings for the letters when they are repeated, you cannot escape the truth of each conclusion. The patterns are *valid,* and when the first two propositions are true, the conclusion has to be true. These are patterns of argument that each of us uses often in daily life, sometimes to convince others of the truth of one of our conclusions, but probably more often just to figure out things that we want to know about. And as we use them we are probably pretty unconscious of the part they are playing in our conversation or inner discourse.

Notice that in the "primed" version of the patterns, where wording has been assigned to the patterns, in the part of the argument giving evidence for the conclusion all the statements are true, according to common knowledge. (Except the statement about Alice Hogan, which is not common knowledge. Please trust me on that one.) The statements in the patterns, using letters instead of the names of real things, are neither true nor false, but merely represent possible propositions that could, in their own right, be true (or false*) once the names of real things have been substituted in for the symbolic letters.

Let's have a diversion for a moment with an example of an argument in which a word *does not* mean the same thing when it is used a second time:

Rolling Stone is a magazine.
A magazine is a place where explosives are kept.
Therefore, *Rolling Stone* is a place where explosives are kept.

Silly, isn't it? But if the difference between the first and the second appearance of the ambiguous word is only slight, then it can be misleading, as can be seen in the next example:

In his acts of protest, Harry was very determined.
Determined actions are those that are caused by something outside the individual and are not done of his own free will.
Therefore, Harry in his acts of protest was not acting of his own free will.

This indeed could be misleading, especially to a reader or hearer who is not very cautious about what he or she accepts. The first occurrence of the word *determined* means "resolute, stubborn, unyielding." The second means "fixed by antecedent causes so as to leave no alternative." As written, however, the argument may seem to use the word in the same sense in each position, leading to conscious or unconscious confusion in the reader or hearer.†

Valuative arguments can be built in the same ways as factual arguments, with the understanding that there are limitations and necessary cautions. Let's repeat some previously seen examples and examine some new ones.

---

*If the opening statements in the examples were false, or contained nonsense words, then the conclusions would be worthless.

†Another sort of factual argument, the *inductive argument,* will be brought in briefly toward the end of the next chapter on valuative arguments. It does not belong in this chapter, which is about *valid* arguments, because it does not have the possibility of being valid.

A. All a are b.
   All b are c.
   Therefore, all a are c.

A". All chocolate malts are drinks made with chocolate.
    All drinks made with chocolate are delicious drinks.
    Therefore, all chocolate malts are delicious drinks.

B. All a are b.
   Smith is a.
   Therefore, Smith is b.

B". All successful generals are excellent tacticians.
    Norman Schwarzkopf is a successful general.
    Therefore, Norman Schwarzkopf is an excellent tactician.

C. If proposition P is true, then proposition Q is true.
   If proposition Q is true, then proposition R is true.
   Therefore, if proposition P is true, then proposition R is true.

C". If you find a stray dog that obviously belongs to someone,
    then you ought to take the dog into your care.
    If you take the dog into your care, then you ought to feed it.
    Thus, if you find a stray dog that obviously belongs to some-
    one, then you ought to feed it.

D. If proposition P is true, then proposition Q is true.
   Proposition P *is* true.
   Therefore, proposition Q *is* true.

D". If a soldier wears a sharpshooter's badge, then he is an ex-
    cellent marksman.
    That soldier is wearing a sharpshooter's badge.
    Therefore, that soldier is an excellent marksman.

Examples A", B", C", and D" are all valuative arguments.
What makes them such is the fact that for a conclusion they have
a proposition that is a value claim.

Important: In order for those valuative arguments to be logically *valid*—which they are—an extra requirement is made of them, namely, that *at least one of the premises must be a value claim*. If you'll check them, you'll find that to be the case.

Here is a point on which many logicians may part company with me. In putting a value claim into a formal argument as a premise, we are dropping out the consideration of *truth*.* And, of course, in getting a value claim for a conclusion, we are getting a proposition that is neither true nor false. Nevertheless, if we have properly constructed our argument, the *pattern* is still the same as that of the argument patterns that we call valid. We cannot legitimately say that our conclusion is true, but we can say that it is just as believable as the value claim that we put into it as a premise.

In chapter 24 we will apply the information contained in this chapter, for the purpose of understanding how to convince other people of our own value judgments.

---

*The traditional logicians are still maintaining that truth is one of the defining characteristics of the proposition, and cannot be dropped out. They say that what we do in testing a valuative argument is to tentatively assume the truth of the value claim(s) involved. I, on the other hand, see no harm in recognizing the special nature of value claims, that they just don't have either truth or falsity as one of their properties. I'd rather recognize that, than continue to believe that they are all either true or false but that we can never find out which.

23

Some Unproductive Valuative Arguments

Have you now gotten a good strong impression of how a factual conclusion may be drawn from factual propositions? How, once the conditions for it are strictly met, the conclusion simply *does* follow from the premises? And have you looked over the four conclusions of the examples expressed in propositions (chapter 22, examples A', B', C', and D') to see that they, like their premises, are *fact-claiming* propositions?

Very well, then, let us look at some arguments that arrive at (or are thought to arrive at) *value-claiming* propositions.

THE *IS-OUGHT* FALLACY

1. All Klackas County citizens turn on their headlights when driving in the rain.

Clint Colston is a Klackas County citizen.
Therefore, Clint Colston ought to turn on his headlights when driving in the rain.

Did you ever hear anyone argue like this? There's a certain plausibility to it, but actually the whole argument is totally invalid. It switches from *what does* happen (all Klackas County citizens switch on their headlights) and *is* (Clint Colston is a Klackas County citizen) to *what ought to* happen (Clint Colston ought to turn on his headlights). The premises, the first two propositions, are factual assertions: they don't say anything about *what ought to be*. Yet there it is in the conclusion. But how can a conclusion get any support from some premises, if the premises don't say anything about that conclusion? Obviously, it cannot.

Incidentally, the first premise (if this were a real-life rather than an imaginary situation) is probably false. If it were true, its statement would include Clint Colston, who is said in the second premise to be a citizen of Klackas County. So if the first premise were true, there would be no point in an argument that appears to be an obvious attempt to get the exception (Clint) to conform to the practice of the majority.

The argument is an example of the *is-ought* fallacy. The fallacy consists of taking statements about the way things are, about "the nature of things," and going from recognition of the way they are to the judgment that they *ought* to be that way. The poet Alexander Pope was probably about half wrong, and *very* unwise, to say "Whatever is, is right." There *are* poor people, homeless people, prejudiced people, people with painful and terminal diseases—but surely you will agree that their existence doesn't constitute the way things *ought to be*.

The following is an argument, implicitly contained in a single sentence, that commits the *is-ought* fallacy.

2. According to figures provided by the Alumni Office at [this college] and at other academically comparable schools, the

percentage of our alumni participating in on-campus activities is too low. (From an alumni newspaper)

We might call this the Statistical Division of the Is-Ought Fallacy. It affirms that the way it *is* (at those other schools) is the way it *ought to be* (at our school). Without saying so in words, the statement suggests that by some statistical measure ("figures"), at selected other colleges a greater percentage of alumni on average participate in on-campus activities than at our school. The statement also carries a suggested or implicit premise that is a value claim: "Our alumni *ought to* participate in on-campus activities as much as the alumni of the selected colleges do."

We hear often of "statistical norms," and often see conclusions such as the above drawn from them. But let it be remembered that statistical norms don't emerge as such out of the statistics. Rather, they are designated as norms by human beings who are applying the statistics. Statistics by themselves do not supply, or convert into, value judgments.

It may be legitimate for the school concerned, based on the above-mentioned figures, to take steps to entice more alumni onto the campus for activities. But the program to do so should, I think, be supported by a careful examination of the selected "academically comparable schools" and the nature of the on-campus activities which draw alumni; the number of alumni living within reasonable travel distance to the campus; and a careful statement and criticism of the hidden value-claiming premise, "Our alumni *ought to* participate . . . as much as [those] alumni. . . ." Perhaps reasons for upholding this otherwise uncriticized assumption could be found. Or perhaps it would even be found that "our own" alumni who are in a position to do so are doing better, proportionally, than those of the selected colleges.

Here are some further examples of arguments containing the *is-ought* fallacy.

3. "Churches in our denomination have always been of colonial-style architecture. So we should build our new church in colonial style, too."

The "thinking" here is: What they have always been is what they ought to be.

4. Electrician's supervisor: "The national code calls for installing the ground pole up. How come you are installing all the ground poles down?"

Journeyman electrician: "That's the way we've always done it."

The journeyman's thinking is, "Ground poles down is the way it always has been; therefore, that's the way it ought to be."

5. "Henry! You can't write it into your will that you want to be put into your coffin naked! Why should you ever think such a thing?"

"Why, naked was the way I came into the world, so naked is the way I ought to go out of it."

Henry thinks that he is naked by nature, so he ought to be naked in his last earthly appearance.

6. "Charlie, you still smoke like a smudge pot. Haven't you read how bad smoking is for your health?"

"Yes, but I've always smoked, ever since I was old enough. So I shouldn't give it up now."

Do you have any problem with that one?

7. "Carrie, why do you have a whiskey every day before lunch?"

"Well, Louie always used to have one, and when we got married, I started having one with him."

"But Louie's been dead for ten years!"

"Yes, but we always used to have one, so I think I ought to go on having one now."

Or with that one? But maybe to be charitable to Carrie, we should give her the benefit of the doubt and interpret her fallacious premise as an attempt to tell us that she reverently drinks a toast each day to Louie's memory. Her words don't look that way, but it might be what she really means. It would be kind to Carrie to help her find what her own thoughts actually are, so that she can possibly make a valid argument from them.

To avoid making the *is-ought* fallacy even in situations where it does indeed seem "natural" to do so, we may remind ourselves of the special rule for valuative arguments that we formulated in the previous chapter: To be valid, *an argument having a value-claiming proposition as its conclusion must have at least one value-claiming proposition as a premise.*

Let's rewrite a few of the above arguments accordingly, to see whether they lend themselves to valid argument.

8. All Klackas County citizens ought to turn on their headlights when driving in the rain.
   Clint Colston is a Klackas County citizen.
   Therefore, Clint Colston ought to turn on his headlights when driving in the rain.

This argument is *valid.* Notice that the new first premise is a value-claiming proposition. We can readily identify the kind of *ought*-judgment it contains: it is a prudential *ought*-judgment. As a valuative proposition it *cannot* be *either* true *or* false, but one can either agree or disagree with it. And since the argument is valid in form, if one agrees with the first premise (and accepts the second, factual, premise), one is therefore compelled to agree with its conclusion.

But there's one more thing. You probably had an impression that although the argument is valid, it just doesn't say as much as the earlier argument (example 1), the one containing the fallacy. Of course it doesn't. If somebody who is trying to get Clint Colston to use his headlights in the rain could do so by using this weaker argument form, he wouldn't be impelled, or deceived, into trying to use the argument that sounds stronger but is not valid. This circumstance often arises, in situations where someone is trying to prove a value judgment by the invalid method of stating what the facts are and drawing a conclusion using the assumption that the way it *is* is the way it *ought to be*. We'll soon look at what to do about that—at the question of how to make the strongest arguments that we can when we want to prove a value-claiming proposition.

9. You always ought to install electrical equipment the way the national electricians' code calls for.
The code calls for installing outlets with ground poles up.
Therefore, you ought to install outlets with ground poles up.

A clear, valid argument, isn't it? Notice how this argument secures the acceptance of whoever it is that is receiving it—the journeyman electrician, for example. The strategy is to offer a *broad, general value assertion* to which the receiver of the argument almost certainly consents. Then show him how the specific case fits within that broad assertion. This method is one of only a very few that can be helpful in supporting value-claiming conclusions. It is further demonstrated in chapter 24.

10. All churches in our denomination ought to be of colonial-style architecture.
We are about to build a new church.
Therefore, we ought to make the new church in colonial-style architecture.

This argument is valid. The first premise is value-claiming, and so is the conclusion. The second premise is fact-claiming. The conclusion does *not* introduce any terms or ideas that were not present in the evidence given for it, the premises.

I am *not* saying that it is always wrong when something is done in the way it has always been done, or in the way that a knowledge of its nature and past history tells us it has been done. There are times when there are good reasons for continuing with an established way of doing things rather than adopting a new way.

For example:

11. People in our part of the country have always associated churches of a colonial style of architecture with our denomination.
    We ought to select a style of architecture for our new church that people will associate with our denomination.
    Therefore, we ought to select the colonial style of architecture for our new church.

Perhaps this argument brings out into the open thoughts that the speaker in the third example was working with without knowing it.

Next is a case showing an appeal to the way things are when there is good reason to do so, rather than mere laziness, ignorance, or indifference to the quality of thinking.

12. In a city with a beach where driving was permitted, a veterinarian noticed that some dog owners were exercising their dogs by running them on the beach with a leash fastened to the owner's moving car.
    The veterinarian put a message in the local newspaper, addressed to these dog owners, warning them that it was injurious to the dogs to run them in this fashion. "That," he said, "is not their natural pace." Dogs don't naturally run steadily for long distances, he went on, and they shouldn't be made to do so because it can injure them severely.

The veterinarian is not making the *is-ought* fallacy. Rather, he has consulted his special knowledge and seen that there is good reason, in the existing nature of dogs, not to exercise the dog by using a car. Dogs should be exercised in a way that uses their natural pace, consisting of bursts of speed interspersed with stops, not simply because they always have exercised that way (which would be the *is-ought* fallacy), but because their bone and muscle structures and physical systems are adapted to running with interruptions, not steadily (the good reason).

INDUCTIVE ARGUMENTS

The arguments we have so far studied are of the kind called *deductive*. These use one or two premises to lead to a conclusion such that if the premise(s) is (are) true, the conclusion must be true. The other main kind of argument is called the *inductive* argument. We are most familiar with it in the form of *generalization*. The reason it is useful is not that its conclusion is guaranteed true, but rather that it is in some degree *probable*. Its premises cover instances that have been examined; but its conclusion, being a general statement, covers not only those but also instances that have not been examined. What one knows after reaching an inductive conclusion is that the unexamined instances will *probably* be like what the inductive conclusion says they are like, based on the examined instances.

13. A woman who wants a face-lift to improve her personal appearance makes some phone calls to find out from various surgeons what they charge. She keeps a list of her results:

    Dr. Alastair charges over five hundred dollars.
    Dr. Hasty charges over five hundred dollars.
    Dr. Pugwash charges over five hundred dollars.
    Dr. Minkowsky charges over five hundred dollars.
    Dr. Detlov charges over five hundred dollars.
    Dr. Lazarone charges over five hundred dollars.

After her sixth phone call, the woman summarizes her findings with the statement: "Every surgeon I called charges over five hundred dollars."

Finally, she draws a conclusion, inductively, from these specific instances: "It must be that all surgeons who do face-lifts charge over five hundred dollars."

This kind of reasoning obviously is not so airtight as deductive reasoning, and therefore we don't apply the adjective *valid* to its conclusions, even when the arguments are well put together. It is useful precisely because it uses the known cases to tell us about the unknown cases; but then if there are unknown cases and a statement is made about them, that statement obviously could be wrong. Ideally, when we have results reached by inductive generalization, we continue to investigate instances until we have covered all instances that there are, and when and if we reach that point, our knowledge is no longer inductive but simply descriptive.

Argument 13 is an example of a fact-assertive inductive argument. Let's construct one that is value-assertive:

14. Green ought to leave his car in gear when he parks it at work.
    Callaway ought to leave her car in gear when she parks it at the supermarket.
    Rev. Marston ought to leave her car in gear when she parks it at church.
    Principal Horner ought to leave his car in gear when he parks it at school.
    Ma Borden ought to leave her car in gear when she gets home from doing errands.
    Thus everyone ought to leave his/her car in gear when he/she parks it.

I'm not much impressed. It is hard to see this sample argument, or any sample inductive value-claiming argument I've been able to imagine, as being very useful. It is unlikely that anyone needs all those value judgments in the premises, to arrive at a general value claim as a conclusion. Again, I doubt that anyone trying to convince another of a halfway important value judgment could get that other person first to agree that all the premises were believable, even if many could be found. It's good to know that an inductive valuative argument *can* be constructed according to the usual inductive pattern, but for practical purposes I think we can let it go at that.

Thus the inductive argument is rarely productive for reaching value-claiming conclusions. Using it does not commit a fallacy, like using a deductive argument embodying the *is-ought* fallacy or any of the various other fallacies that occasionally creep into deductive arguments. The point is that with these brief explanations, you now know enough about both kinds of reasoning to be able to criticize your own and others' arguments that lead to value-claiming conclusions.

24

How to Convince Others of Your Value Judgments: The First Way

The serious reader by this time has become aware that he or she needs to pose two very important questions concerning value claims:

1. When I want others to believe a value claim that I have adopted, how can I get them to do it?

2. If value claims depend on the judgment of the people who originate them, how can I decide which value claims to believe?

We will address the first question in this and the following chapter, and the second question in chapter 26.

The Romans had a saying, "There is no disputing about tastes." Of course the Romans knew that there were plenty of disputes, verbal quarrels—what most people (but not the logicians) call *arguments*—about matters of taste, such as whether the building called the Pantheon was as beautiful as the Parthenon, or whether the plays of Plautus were as well written as those of Ter-

171

ence. What they most certainly must have meant by their saying is that there is *no hope of resolving* disputes about matters of taste; therefore, it is pointless to debate them.

It is pointless to debate about tastes because tastes are expressed in value judgments, and value judgments—value-claiming propositions—represent no existing realm for us to turn to and inspect, to establish them as true or false. You and another person can agree ever so fully on what the facts are, that is, on which of the fact-claiming propositions are true, and yet simply judge differently. The proposition "spinach is bitter" reports a factual matter that you can both agree upon. The judgment, "the bitterness of spinach is good (= delicious, pleasant)" is not in the factual realm, and has no higher standing than "the bitterness of spinach is bad (= foul-tasting, unpleasant)." This is the way it is with matters of taste, and with all value judgments, of which judgments of taste are examples.

These things being said, it may make you wonder how logic could have any beneficial effect on the situation at all. But we'll find that even in these subjective situations it can be put to good use.

According to a centuries-old tradition in logic, deductive arguments depend for their force upon being constructed correctly. If a deductive argument is constructed in one of the right forms, it is valid. However, validity isn't the same thing as truth. Even a valid argument can have a false conclusion—because, for example, of having a false premise. But the idea of truth is useful in a test of whether an argument is valid; and in logic the following principle is used to define validity:

> A deductive argument is *valid* when it is formed in such a way that, *if* its premise is (or premises are) true, then its conclusion is *true,* and cannot be otherwise.

To illustrate:

1. All apes are primates.
   All primates are mammals.
   Therefore, all apes are mammals.

Another illustration:

2. If a national holiday falls on a Friday or a Monday, government
   employees have a long weekend.
   In January 1994 Martin Luther King, Jr., Day fell on a Monday.
   Therefore, in January 1994 government employees had a long
   weekend.

Now I should like to introduce something else, which I anticipate
will give you no difficulty whatever. Look at this structure:

3. All a are b.
   All b are c.
   Therefore, all a are c.

Isn't it just like argument 1 above?

Well, it's *almost* like argument 1, with the exception of one
thing. It doesn't say anything concrete: its key "words" are mere
symbols, placeholders.

What argument 3 is, is a symbolic structure that *represents* argument 1. It's an argument form that could also represent an in-
finity of other arguments of the same construction. My point is that
(check me on this!) you can follow the reasoning, the logic, of that
argument *even though it doesn't say anything* about specific, concrete things in the real world that you and I inhabit, the world of
apes and primates and government employees and holidays.

Now let's try something that is a little—but not much—different.

4. If the parcel was delivered safely, then Parkins owes money to
   the store.
   The parcel *has* been delivered safely.
   Therefore, Parkins does owe money to the store.

Now here I've tried to pull a fast one on you. You are probably ready to state, on your own knowledge, that the first two premises of argument 1 are true. Apes, you'd say, *are* primates, and primates *are* mammals, and that can be verified by looking the words up in a dictionary. But what about the premises of the second argument. *Was* the parcel delivered safely? (What parcel?) Does that oblige Parkins to pay money to the store? (Who's Parkins? What store?) The best you can say is that *if* Parkins was obliged to pay upon safe arrival, and *if* the parcel did arrive safely, then Parkins now owes money to the store. But when you first read the argument about Parkins, you probably *assumed* that the first two premises were true, and on that assumption you could see the *validity,* the force, of the conclusion even though you actually didn't know whether the premises were true or false.

What I am trying to show you is that the patterns of *validity,* the structures of arguments that are *valid,* are visible in the form not only of valid arguments about actual, real things, but also in the form of abstract patterns (like "All a are b") as well as of *fictional* arguments, where we suspend belief about whether the persons indicated really exist or the events mentioned ever happened. So: *If we can reason validly about abstractions presented in language, and about fictions presented in language, there can be no obstacle to our reasoning validly about conceptions in language of the way things ought to be,* whether they actually are that way or are only present to us in our imagination.

Now in what I believe should be added to the logical tradition, we should keep all the provisions of this sort of everyday logic; but we now recognize that there are value-claiming propositions as well as fact-claiming propositions, and that value-claiming propositions may occasionally be the conclusions of deductive arguments. Validity itself is not affected by this circumstance; we can still have valid arguments when those value-claiming propositions are the conclusions. But the abstract quality called truth *is* affected, for, as you've known for a long time now, the value-claiming propositions do not have that quality; they are neither true nor false. Since they are still meaningful, however, we can arrange them in the forms of valid arguments.

It is from these things that the rule follows, that for a deductive argument having a value-claiming proposition as its conclusion to be *valid,* it must contain at least one value-claiming proposition (not the same one, of course) in the premises.

To illustrate:

5. A growing child ought to drink at least a pint of milk every day.
   Gene Dempsey is a growing child.
   Therefore, Gene Dempsey ought to drink at least a pint of milk every day.

This is a deductive argument in a valid form. If there *is* a person named Gene Dempsey who is a growing child, then the second premise is true. The first premise is a value-claiming proposition expressing somebody's value judgment. As a value-claiming proposition it cannot be true (or false), but it is highly believable, at least in our culture. Since the argument form is valid, we may say that the conclusion, too, is highly believable.

Basically, there are two ways to attempt to bring others to the same value belief that you yourself hold. One of the ways may be better for some of the issues that you discuss, and the second way better for others. While different people will prefer either one way or the other, it is advisable to be well acquainted with both.

The First Way: *Construct a valid deductive argument* that has your value belief as a conclusion, and build the argument so that its conclusion is *based on a pertinent value-claiming proposition* as a premise. Thus you now have one of the answers to the question "How can I convince other people of my value judgments?"

But, wait! you may ask. What about that value-assertive premise? If it cannot be true (just as it cannot be false), why should the other person be convinced?

A way he will be convinced, when you have chosen this method for convincing him, is by his *already believing* the value-assertive proposition that you include as a premise. So it's a good thing to know what your listener already believes in. If he firmly believes in your value-claiming premise, and you have success-fully crafted a valid argument, he will have no choice but to be-lieve your value-claiming conclusion. He will, that is, unless he stops being rational.

It's high time, isn't it, for another illustration:

6. All persons ought to be permitted to conduct their private lives as they wish, so long as they harm no one.

   Joe Helmboldt is a person.

   Therefore, Joe Helmboldt ought to be permitted to conduct his private life as he wishes, so long as he harms no one.

Do you see the validity of this argument? If the two premises were true, the conclusion would have to be true. However, since the value-claiming premise that opens the argument can be neither true nor false, but is *believed* by our adversary in a debate over permissible behavior, then (if he is going to remain rational), he will have to believe the conclusion equally strongly.

Now in a real-life situation, sometimes your adversary will see the necessary rational conclusion and will adopt your value as-sertion as a belief of his own. So you have succeeded. But on the other hand, your argument may make him focus on the value-claiming premise that your argument uses, and he'll decide that he doesn't believe it after all. So he shifts his ground. And then you have to start over. But at least you have made something clear to him, and yourself, about what his beliefs actually are. Perhaps you make a mental note to look out for this person's inconsistencies.

Possibly you can find some value claims that nearly every-body believes, to use in arguments concluding with a value claim. What about these:

7. One ought never to leave a child alone in the presence of something very dangerous.

8. Everyone ought to pay his fair share of the taxes to support the government.

9. A nation's government ought to maintain the conditions of peace and order on which the citizen's safety depends.

Are those pretty widely believed? Can you add to the list?

Perhaps you can. But your problem is finding such a proposition, believed by nearly everyone, that fits into the argument for a value claim that you are trying to get others to believe.

Suppose you are trying to convince someone that your community ought not to extend a temporary tax-free status to a big new business, Duf-L-Bags International, that is thinking about moving in. In such a case you might say that Duf-L-Bags International ought to pay full taxes rather than be tax-exempt, because (your premise) everyone ought to pay his fair share of the taxes that support the government, and (another premise) Duf-L-Bags International is simply a corporation, a "corporate person," no different from other companies already present that pay their fair share. The first premise is a value claim (see example 8). The second premise is factual.

In real life, some people are in favor of tax breaks for industries moving into an area, while others oppose them. What the argument makes us realize, once it is set out clearly, is that anybody who favors the tax breaks in spite of example 8 above, does not really believe that "everyone ought to pay his fair share of taxes to support his government." If he supports tax-exempt status for Duf-L-Bags International, he is taking exception to that general principle. Pointing this out could put the opponent of tax breaks in a strong position, because in a democracy, it is difficult not to be in favor of equality.

Now, where did we derive the value assertion that everyone ought to pay his fair share of taxes?

When the Founding Fathers wrote the Declaration of Independence, they included the idea that a government ought to bring about the safety and happiness of the governed, and they called this a self-evident truth. Since that time we have become rather suspicious of claims of what is a self-evident truth. To some people, it is a self-evident truth that "I ought to get everything I need first, and after that you can get some of the things you need, if there's anything left." Such a principle might be enunciated in a shipwreck-on-a-desert-island scenario. However, we are in a position something like that of the Founding Fathers in our attempts to find value assertions on which there will be wide agreement, or even on which our particular opponent will agree with us. That is, we are in a position in which we have a value claim that has somehow found its way into our consciousness: we like it, we believe other persons ought to believe it, but we know neither how we got it nor how we can support it. It just "looks right," as if we and everyone else ought to believe it. In a word, it is a "self-evident truth"—we think.

But if *I* were to end up thinking that, I would say that I must not have checked something as thoroughly as I should have. Having an inkling that a value-claiming conclusion is still not to be believed is a likely sign that one has subconsciously noticed a flaw that he has not yet elucidated or put into words. I'd think it over a great deal more.

25

How to Convince Others of
Your Value Judgments: The Second Way

Reflect for a moment on how you arrive at your own value judgments. Of course, as a child you tended to accept the value beliefs that your parents and other respected persons presented to you, but eventually education freed you from being dependent upon those. After that, how did you do it?

The way we ordinarily get *our own* value judgments, when we are not simply accepting the value assertions of others, is to *survey the facts,* and then to make our own valuative judgment, comparing or contrasting the facts with the way that, in our opinion, things ought to be. We may have a preconception of how things ought to be, or we may have to work at it until one emerges from our survey of the facts.

Here is an example of how I might arrive at a practical value judgment about how to move a piece of furniture.

I am (let us say) trying to move a file cabinet from the corner of my study to a place beside the door. I lock the cabinet, so that the drawers will stay shut, then I grasp one of the drawer handles and pull. I succeed in moving the cabinet a few inches. But then I see that I have scraped the hardwood floor and left a scar where the corner of the cabinet moved across it. I judge, on seeing the scar, "That's not the way it ought to be."

I think further: If I keep on moving the cabinet this way, I'll make more scars on the floor. And there ought not to be scars on the floor. If I drag the cabinet on a furniture pad, or if I put wheels under it somehow, I can move it without putting scars on the floor. And I have an old quilt in the garage that I can use as a furniture pad.

And finally: I ought to go get the quilt, put it under the cabinet, and move the cabinet that way.

Thus I make a value judgment *after a survey of the facts*. I "see for myself" how things are, then make up my mind.

That incident exemplifies a pretty simple sort of arrival at one's own value judgment—one's judgment of how things ought to be.

Now I'm on my way back from the garage with the quilt under one arm. My domestic partner challenges me: "Stop!" she says. "What are you doing with my good quilt?"

I explain that I need to use it a few minutes in my study.

"Why on earth?"

"To move my file cabinet."

"Well, can't you just move your file cabinet, without keeping it warm with my quilt?"

"Come look. I'll show you why I need the quilt."

So I have her go with me to the study and look at the dislocated file cabinet, then at the scar on the floor. "You see, I have to have something for a pad under the file cabinet, so I won't do any more of that."

"All right, but don't get it dirty, and don't tear it, and. . . ."

Thus by putting the facts of the case before her eyes, I have brought her to judge the same way I do, that the file cabinet ought to be moved by using the quilt.

Sometimes the purpose is not to reach a judgment of the form, "Here's what you ought to do," as in the incident just given, but simply to arrive at a value judgment where there was none before, or perhaps to improve a preexisting value judgment, to be kept in one's store of beliefs.

Suppose you and I are visiting the National Gallery of Art in Washington, D.C., and we come to a painting by Picasso. I stop before it, and I frown. You, on the other hand, look with admiration on the picture and call Picasso a "master." This is assuredly a value judgment, and a favorable one.

"Master?" I reply. "How come? It looks pretty confused to me."

"Ah, but that's part of it!" you exclaim. "He wants to show you that out of the confusion of daily existence, certain fine relationships emerge. See how no single color or shade, except black, appears on more than one object. That makes color an important element of the picture. And see how it makes the musical instrument, which is a bright red, stand out. Now the other thing that is conspicuously bright is the white paper of sheet music. That's telling you that you should be expecting harmony. And yet it's ambiguous whether that is really sheet music after all, because the lines on it could also be stanzas of poetry. And notice how when you survey all the interesting things that are there—the thing that is maybe a bottle or a statuette, the pair of boots, the bird—you begin to wonder what supports it all. And only then do you realize that there is a table underneath it all. It hardly looks like a table, just a long, straight brown rectangle like a piece of mahogany, but you know it must be the edge of the table because there is a chair pushed up to it. And the chair is both the most graceful and the most traditional object in the painting. Everything else is hardedged and crisp, contrasting with the softness and smooth curving lines of the chair. And the clutter on the table dominates not only the table but the whole corner of the room, showing that the person who lives there doesn't care for the grace and beauty of the chair, or anything it stands for. Now, do you see why Picasso is a master?"

My first reaction is to think of asking, "You mean, you see all of that in that painting?" But I save myself from saying such a stupid thing, because the painting is before us, and *we are both looking at exactly the same thing.* As I gaze further at the painting, I *do* note that the banjo, or mandolin, or guitar, or whatever it is, is bright red and dominates the picture. Yes, the lines on the (presumed) paper could be stanzas, as well as lines of musical notation. The bird looks pretty artificial; he could be stuffed, or even a cutout picture. The curvy-edged object could be a Coke bottle or a statuette of a voluptuous lady. Everything you've said is factually true of the painting.

The only thing you've said that is not a fact claim is your summation: "Picasso is a master."

The upshot is that you have taught me more than I knew before about how to survey the pertinent facts, and after I have learned that and done that, *I judge the same way that you do,* that Picasso is indeed a master. He paints the way that someone who has his kind of concern to get across ought to paint. This incident *illustrates my arrival at a particular judgment by a direct survey of the facts.*

More often we use a more complex pattern that brings together direct experience and information already gathered, which are expressed in statements based on memory or obtained through research. There follows a typical example of this more complex pattern.

Let us imagine that you are urging a neighbor of yours to try out for the Olympics in diving. How do you decide that he is of Olympic caliber? By watching him dive, right? You watch the athlete, and watch others and compare his performance with theirs. You have probably been watching divers for quite a while, before you consider yourself qualified to suggest anybody for the Olympics. You also recall TV coverage of Olympic divers during the actual games.

Along with this, you have probably been reading current newspaper sports pages and sports magazines, finding facts about other divers and their skills, and certainly this activity enhances your ability to judge well, to judge that a given performer is of Olympic quality. Perhaps you also have talked with other fans of the same sport. You frame for yourself a general knowledge of the sport of diving.

From this you decide that your neighbor performs well enough to be competitive with others who might try out for the Olympic Games.

Thus, when we form our own value judgments from the facts themselves, we survey them on two levels. The first level is that of direct experience: We watch, in this case, the performer himself. This is *direct observation of the facts of the situation.* The second level is acquainting ourselves with information supplied by other people. From their reports, both their fact-claiming statements and their value claims, we increase our knowledge about what we are adjudging. This is *use of preexisting information.*

These incidents illustrate the way we arrive at value judgments of our own. From them we can see what is the second way to convince others of our value claims.

The Second Way: *Gather the facts that made you judge as you did,* that made *you* arrive at that value-claiming proposition as one of your own beliefs. *Draw your listener's attention to these facts,* in the same form as that in which you judged them—that is, direct observation or the statements of others, or both—*and ask him to judge for himself.*

In most situations, chances are good that your listener will judge the same way as you did. However, if he does not, and if you have been thorough, there is nothing further you can do to convince him, and the two of you will do well simply to agree to disagree.

Thus you now have two ways of convincing someone else to believe your value judgment. The first method obviously uses deductive reasoning. The second method closely resembles inductive reasoning, but is not the same thing. It is inductive in approach, but it does not use the same mechanism of reasoning, namely generalization. Rather, it uses that mysterious and distinctly human action, the making of a value judgment.

26

Testing the Value Claims of Others

Now that we have sketched the ways in which we could persuade others to agree with us in our own value claims, we can see how to examine others' value judgments and to decide whether or not to accept them. It is with the same methods, applied in reverse.

Let's call the person who is offering us a value judgment "the advocate."

The first thing to do is to survey the case that the advocate is offering us. Has he identified the value judgment, and clearly stated it in an unambiguous value-claiming proposition for us? If not, we'd better help him do that, so that both of us will agree on what it is we're talking about.

Now, what is the advocate depending on to convince us? Is it a simple relation between his value claim and one or two or (rarely) more propositions? If so, he is probably using a deductive argument. Or, on the other hand, is he presenting a body of factual statements or having us look at the physical facts, assuming that we will judge the same way that he judges? Then he's using the "see for yourself" method, our "second way."

Here, then, are some instructions to use if the advocate is using the first method to support his judgment—that is, instructions for testing a deductive argument that has a value claim for its conclusion.

1. Identify the conclusion, filling it out if necessary. Then identify the propositions that serve as premises for the conclusion, those statements that, taken alone or together, provide evidence for warranting the concluding value claim.

2. Decide which premise, if any, is a value- claiming proposition. If there is no value-claiming proposition among the premises, you will know that the argument is not in a valid form, and does not provide a reason for believing the conclusion. Quite likely, the argument embodies the *is-ought* fallacy.

3. When you have found a value-claiming proposition as a premise, decide whether it is *acceptable to you,* one that you can *believe.*

4. If the argument meets all the above criteria, then test its structure to ascertain whether it is valid (for there are, of course, other reasons such an argument can be invalid besides its offering a valuative conclusion without a value claim among its premises). If you've studied deductive logic, you'll know how to do this thoroughly, by the rules of inference used in logic to show the progression of reasoning from premises to conclusion. If you haven't, carefully tracing the argument through will probably give you an intuition as to its validity or invalidity.

If you do not find the value-claiming premise acceptable, then you surely have no reason by virtue of the argument to accept the conclusion. If you find that the value-claiming premise is conditionally acceptable to you, then you can conditionally accept the conclusion. If you find the premise to be indubitable, then you are rationally compelled to regard that the conclusion is indubitable as well. (And if you don't feel so compelled, look the argument over again with great suspicion.)

With regard to the second way, the "see for yourself" way, you simply reverse roles with the advocate. Now he is in the place you formerly held (see chapter 25) when you were using the second way to convince someone else, and you take the place of the person whom somebody is trying to convince. You give him every opportunity to exhibit or state facts to you, and when he is finished, you make your own judgment. Thus even if later a witness should say, "The advocate convinced him/her (you, the reader)," it will be by virtue of *your own ability to judge* that you come to hold the same belief as the advocate. Once we recognize this, we see that there is no reason to be ashamed of following someone else's lead in arriving at a given value judgment. We are not failing to be original in our thinking.

Much the greater number of cases are those in which the advocate does not show us concrete physical facts but depends entirely upon his statements of fact. There are two possible kinds of weakness that his argument might suffer from: one is in the statements of facts offered, the other has to do with the value judging itself.

The advocate's fact-claiming propositions, expressing those things on which he makes his judgment, must be as nearly perfect as possible, clearly expressed and free of misstatements. One way to oppose his judgment legitimately is to challenge fact-claiming statements that we don't believe to be true. The advocate may have a preliminary job to do, i.e., to prove some of his factual assertions on which he bases his valuative judgment, before he can bring in his value-claiming conclusion and claim that we should agree with it.

A difference in our perceptions of the *facts* can weaken an advocate's case. If the advocate cannot put to rest our doubts about his statements of fact, we would do well to be reluctant to accept his conclusion. We want to be willing to judge upon the facts as they are, but we don't want to judge upon someone's misperception of the facts.

Moreover, some fact-claiming statements assert probabilities, not established facts. Ideally, the advocate's argument is free of these, but where there is nothing else available for him to use, the advocate should acknowledge that he is using probability statements and qualify his conclusion accordingly. His value-claiming conclusion is weaker because of dependence on probabilities, and generally, the more probabilities used as data, the weaker is the argument for believing the value judgment that is the conclusion.

So much for factual weaknesses in the advocate's case. Are there identifiable factors of weakness of judgment, on which we also could base a refusal to accept his value claim?

At first it seems as though there must be such factors of weak judgment. Most of us firmly believe that some persons are wiser than others, which means that they are better value judges, better creators of value-claiming statements. Yet to turn to them has simply the strength, or the weakness, of the long-known appeal to authority. This is because any effort to establish that the wisdom of A is greater than that of B is itself to make a value judgment. And value judgments, we have long recognized, are not provable. The only thing we can be thrown back upon is *our own* judgment, and with it the appeal to the judgment of other persons besides the advocate, to present to those others the value judgment that the advocate has not judged wisely. We now know better than to seek *proof* by going in this direction, for none lies there. No doubt the best outcome is simply for both parties to agree to disagree. We explore this further in the next chapter.

27

Are There Value Judgments on Value Judgments?

The poet Alfred, Lord Tennyson wrote, " 'Tis better to have loved and lost, than never to have loved at all" (*In Memoriam*). He was expressing his grief over the loss of his friend Arthur Hallam, who died at the age of twenty-two. However, Tennyson was unaware that he was also giving us a good pattern for realizing that there indeed *can* be value judgments upon value judgments, for he was relaying two value judgments to us and setting one with stark clarity above the other. We could (clumsily, in contrast to the liquid syllables of Tennyson) express the compound judgment in the words, "To have loved and lost is more nearly the way things ought to be (or less the way things ought not to be) than never to have loved at all."

The importance of the Tennyson passage to our project is that it demonstrates for us that we can indeed make value judgments upon value judgments. Tennyson says that never to have loved at all is of a certain goodness, a certain degree of value, in being free of the pain that the poet feels; but to have loved and lost, even though it entails pain, is of a greater goodness, a greater value.

Consider this first example:

1. I ought to get rid of those squirrels in the attic. I oughtn't leave any of them dead up there, because that would lead to an unpleasant odor, and I ought not kill any of them anyway if I can solve the problem without killing, because I ought not to take life. But I ought to get them out of there because they are eating up all the chicken feed in the nearby woodshed and they are littering and making a mess in the attic. They chatter all afternoon and prevent Mims from getting a good sleep, and she needs her nap in order to be strong enough to do her work. So I ought to find some way to get rid of the squirrels without killing them.

While this speaker probably hasn't yet made any decision about his action, he has put several *ought*-judgments into a priority list. The top priority is to get rid of the squirrels. The second priority is to do that without killing any of them. The third is to end the chattering that keeps Mims awake. Pursuing the line of reasoning already started, the speaker might say, "It is better to end the chattering than not end the chattering. It is better not to kill the squirrels than to kill them. And it is better to get rid of the squirrels than to let them stay in the attic." Here are three instances of judging one value claim to be better, more the way things ought to be, than another.

The point is that we *actually do* judge value claims. Here is another example.

2. First I thought I ought to have another drink to get my mind off my troubles, but then I thought I ought not to, because I'd be pretty drunk and I ought not to run over anybody when I'm driving home.

Very likely, we all approve the second thought of this speaker, and there seems little debate about which judgment ought to be given preference over the other. Is it true that the drivers who do get drunk and *do* run over people just don't think about options like this one? Or do they consciously decide that the moral duty not to run over anyone while driving drunk does not outweigh the prudential judgment in favor of relieving the mind of its troubles?

I dare say there are very few persons, very few indeed, who would support this speaker in drinking more, to relieve his mind of his troubles, and afterward driving home drunk. But how is it that we make a judgment on a point like that? In this case, we probably say that many more people are likely to be placed in harm's way if the speaker drives home drunk than if he makes the sacrifice to safety of one more drink. This view is predicated on the premise that one should always strive to achieve "the greatest good or least pain for the greatest number." But ethical philosophers are constantly testing that idea (the principle of utility) and as yet have not found a convincing proof why it should be a final principle.

It is fortunate for us that there are opposing values—differing conceptions of the way it ought to be—that are fairly clear, as in our first example, and that are amenable to near-unanimous decision. Sometimes society makes the decision, then hands it down to individuals by means of a law, as when it frowns upon the way Marilyn Pardee dances or makes laws against drunk driving. Societies do actually make value judgments, often imposing them by law upon all who are within that society; but sometimes they omit to express a judgment in law and let individuals deviate from it if they choose—and have the courage. The circumstances to which society responds are generally those in which individuals would do differently than the collective judgment of society calls for—they do what is self-interested rather than other-interested. Either party can express its judgment in value-claiming propositions:

3. A person ought never to drive a vehicle when he or she is intoxicated.

4. A person ought to use the means that are available to relieve his
   or her mind of its troubles.

Seeing these alternatives, any one of us can exert his own judgment, in saying that no. 3 is a better value judgment than no. 4 (or
the other way around, if he chooses).

Are there any rules or instructions that will help us learn to
make better rather than worse value decisions? Largely not. Perhaps a general scheme of these could be drawn up, and in fact quite
a number of the proponents of one or another ethical system do
generate rules and urge their followers to obey them. In this book,
however, I should prefer that we deal with matters in a nonpartisan
way, rather than as utilitarians or deontologists or Kantians or Aris-
totelians or members of some other ethical school of thought, although all these schools are very respectable intellectually.

But rather than default, I should like to say also, from my own
experience and observation of others, especially of those whose
writings I have read, that we *are capable of improving* our ability
to make value judgments. Do you not make better value judgments now than you did in your infancy, your early childhood,
even your teens? It is a rare person who answers no to that question. I do not wish to settle the matter by counting noses or votes;
rather, I think that universal experience, the experience we all
have in this matter, bears out the suggestion that as we grow and
mature, we become better at evaluating.

Problems arise, of course, when there is a value issue between
persons of about the same degree of maturity. If these cannot be
resolved in the ways sketched in previous chapters, we do well (a
value claim of mine!) to live and let live, agree to disagree, agree
that the problem is serious but that no one solution is conclu-
sively more supportable than another. Time, and with it the gathering wisdom of the generations, will help us resolve such issues.

What I am recommending (with my "live and let live" approach) is to place the valuation of life itself above the valuation of the evaluative propositions of either side, indeed of both sides collectively, in those important matters.

Our language has long maintained a distinction between these two concepts, a smart person and a wise person. Both are intelligent. However, a person may be "smart" yet not be wise. He or she may be a "smart businessman," a "smart horsewoman," a "smart hunter," a "smart soccer player" or "street-smart," and yet be merely mediocre or even inferior in the other departments of life. A wise person, on the other hand, seems to conduct his or her own life well, to give very good advice to others when asked, and to be self-content. One may be "smart" in business or smart enough (knowing oneself) not to go into business. He or she probably has certain special interests such as a vocation or physical recreation or hobbies. But it is not these that gain a person the reputation and respect for being wise. What it is, in my opinion, is the ability to make excellent value judgments.

In the next chapter there is a list of eight capabilities that you will have acquired or strengthened in yourself if you have read this book with reasonable care and applied its teachings in your life. To exercise any one of them will almost certainly give you pleasure and a feeling of accomplishment—reason enough to undertake them. It will also tend to create both greater respect from others and a heightened self-respect. The ideal would be to exercise all of them constantly in a blend of practices that enables you to build with values a broader understanding, to sculpt with values a finer structure of the mind. A single step of progress in handling any one of them is a step toward that admirable state called wisdom.

28

What You Can Do Now

It's time to survey our progress. If this cruise through the turbulent waters of values has been a success, there are several things you ought to be able to do now, better than before.

1. *You should be able to identify value judgments, even the heavily camouflaged ones.* A great part, at least half, of this book has been devoted to this purpose. Here I have suggested that identifying value judgments involves certain difficulties, and that a habit of practicing it would be fruitful.

2. *You should be able to get more out of books, articles, and other things you read, as well as speeches and public presentations you hear or see.* When you make "Look for the value judgments!" a rule in what you read, you are very likely to finish with a reasoned response, rather than just a first (but unfortunately also final) impression. You will be able to compare "pro and con" presentations, and do a better job on what candidates to vote for, and which side to take in public issues.

194

3. *You should be able to take a fuller part in discussions in which values are discussed, particularly those in which conflicting values enter.* You may find yourself playing the role of a friendly counselor to others, saying, "Let me ask you—do you believe that such-and-such (an item at issue) is what ought to be done?" and in that way bringing out the ideas of others, when they have a tendency simply to call their ideas their "values" and let that be all the explanation they make.

4. *You should be able to explain values better—particularly to yourself!* You now know how to take a word or phrase that is used to name a value, and translate it into an *ought*-judgment. Thus you can make it say far more clearly what its value is.

5. *You should be able to formulate your own values.* A young person says to herself, "I always have believed in marriage. But come to think of it, what is it exactly that I believe in, when I say I believe in marriage as a value?"

"Now," she goes on, having been a loyal reader of this book, "I know what to do." So she jots down on a scratchpad the words "ought to," then builds several sentences around the phrase:

5a. *"Two young people who love each other deeply ought to get married."* No, that won't do. There are some couples in love who ought not to get married, for one reason or another, for example, if one of them is married already.

5b. *"A young person who wants to live a fulfilled life, even through old age, ought to get married."* No, that's not right, because it isn't all there. Whom are you going to marry—just anybody?

5c. And so she goes on, finally arriving at *"Young people should regard marriage as the ideal personal relationship, should enter it only after adequate physical and psychological preparation, should commit themselves to it fully, and should enter it only with a partner who fully believes in the same values."*

Now, that's better, she says. It's flexible enough to admit different kinds of circumstances and personalities, and can admit loving second marriages, and it contains the idea of full commitment, which is essential. She now feels good about her longtime belief in marriage as a value, and decides to keep her statement as a point in her personal creed, always watching for any further factors that might require her to modify it. With a contented smile, she calls it a job well done.

6. *You should be able to discover new values.* You now know how to express values—say, those of foreign cultures—in language that makes them explicit, and you are developing a habit of thinking about them in terms of what their believers think ought to be done. You might even find yourself doing it some time!

7. *You should be able to place values on a priority scale, so that when a conflict arises among values you yourself accept, you can more confidently place one above another.* For example, the young woman in our fifth example was deciding which values, signaled by their respective *ought*-judgments, ought (yes, ought) to be included in her defining statement for the value "marriage." By striking some out, she was giving them lower priority than those she brought in.

A frequent occasion nowadays for such a process is the discussion between two young people of whether they should get married or simply live together. They can help themselves to resolve it by asking, "If we just live together, are there values of marriage that we will be missing?" and "If we marry, are there values of living together without marriage that we will be missing?"

8. *You should be able to apply the best means of convincing others to believe your value judgments, or else to satisfy yourself that you have at least used every reasonable means to convince them.* You know that there are two systematic ways, described in chapters 24 and 25, for applying the logic of valuative arguments. If

these are not applied, any discussion of a value judgment that someone is urging is likely to be illogical. Now, illogicalness isn't always bad. Some things, poetry for example, may even be improved by it. Most people, however, will prefer their scale of values to be arrived at logically rather than illogically, which is tantamount to being arrived at by no method at all.

9. *You should be able to see life and experience more as a united whole, rather than as a miscellaneous scattering of unequal and often jarring parts, because now you know an all-important way in which the past and the future interrelate.*

Facts belong to the past, and values to the future. They meet in the present. Values are conceptions of the way things ought to be, achievable in the future, and, for many of them, *only* in the future. Facts, belonging to the past and reaching up to the present, are the starting place for the changes that will make real, rather than solely conceptual, the values that we seek to bring about in the future. Our values are the scope of our creativity, our reaffirming or our reshaping of the facts, as we carry out the rest of our lives.

29

Forming Your Most Important
Value Beliefs

It looks probable to me that most persons "acquire their values," that is, acquire the principal value-claiming propositions that they believe, in infancy and in childhood. These are probably arrived at with about as much organization as there is in a child's toy chest. In the process of upbringing, parents usually handle value considerations case by case, not in a systematic fashion. In doing so, they probably only barely suggest an order of priorities for the values that happen to be brought into the cases receiving attention.

For example, a preschooler, Cody, and his little sister, Cassandra, are both tugging on one of Cody's toy trucks. Cody secures possession of the truck by letting go of the toy and hitting Cassandra hard on the side of the head. Their mother hears Cassandra's outcry and comes to adjudicate. In her talk to the children, she shames Cassandra for trying to take a toy without asking permission, and she shames Cody more strongly for resorting to physical force against his little sister. She takes the truck, places it out of reach of both children on a high shelf, and tells each child to play with something else and behave properly toward one another.

This mother is upholding and demonstrating her belief in several values: the right to property of one's own, the impropriety of greed and aggression toward another's property, the right to be free of physical force and the impropriety of applying it without trying other redress, the impropriety of using force against a physically weaker person (the younger Cassandra is smaller than Cody), the impropriety of strife within a family, and the impropriety of a male's striking a female. She has shown that peace is in her view better than conflict. She has thus ranked some of her value beliefs. For example, she has demonstrated to her children that the right of all to peace is more important that the desire to possess a particular material thing. She has shown that she believes proper behavior is compatible with the pleasures of play, but that the "ought's" of proper behavior take precedence over the the playing child's notions of what it would be fun to do.

That's a sizeable collection of value judgments, including some comparisons of value judgments. All those value judgments emerge in the mother's mind from this one little everyday incident involving her children. She hopes, of course, that the children will absorb her value beliefs and conduct themselves in the future according to them. If that dozen or more value beliefs are all implicit in this simple incident, how many more value assertions must we believe in, in order to govern our daily lives!

A very frequent question asked by those who have become aware of the pervasiveness of values in our lives, is "Where ought I to get my value beliefs?"

One ready answer is, you've already got them. You have indeed acquired them mostly from the home and the family circle, just as Cody and Cassandra were doing, incidental to their play. At the age of youthful revolt, you probably acquired some more, and maybe jettisoned some of those you had. And for many people, this is about as far as value development in life goes, and it has been largely an unconscious process. Now, however, you are at an age of discretion, and you may be mindful of Socrates' dictum, "The examined life is the only life worth living." You would do well to question the acquisition of your value beliefs.

However, to start the question with *where* may not be the significant thing. "*How* ought I to get my value beliefs" is broader than "Where . . . ?" as it may include *where* but not be confined to it.

One person I know answered the "where" question with a simple answer: "In church." She said nothing about the great variety of churches and of often conflicting church-fostered beliefs. Others answer, "In the family, first and foremost." These probably depend on the family-inculcated values being strong enough to outcompete peer values, street values, even church values, and whatever other rivals there might be to the "family values." None of these or other answers that circulate in our culture has been so satisfactory that society has adopted it and held it to be absolute. But awareness of the many conflicts in human behavior in our society, as well as awareness that behavior both expresses and is guided by value beliefs, makes our proposed task of leading the examined life extremely important to us, and very perplexing.

"How ought I to get my value beliefs?" Before examining life, let's examine the question, which is itself asking for a value judgment as its answer! And by now we know that if the answer is a value-claiming proposition, it does not partake of the dimension of truth. Hence any answer can only be advisory, not factual. Yet we recognize how vital the question is and how desirable is an answer. We also recognize how important it is to us as individuals to receive good, not bad, advice on this matter. But again, instructing someone to get *good* advice is in turn asking that person to discriminate between good and bad advice, good and bad advisers—in other words, to make a very important value judgment.

What it comes down to is an old, old saying: "Each of us must be his or her own philosopher." For surely a critical examination of one's life is a philosophical pursuit, and no one else is in a better position to examine your life than you are.

There are, so far as I know, no ready answers that will do for all times and all persons, although I don't say that we may not hope to find that blessing in some future era. In chapter 25, I supplied the best answer I have been able to find to the question "How can I test the value claims of others?" To conduct a critical examination of your own life entails that you examine your own value judgments and compare them with those of others, just as it entails examining your own occupational performance, say, and comparing it with others'. Though there is no body of rules to follow for evaluating values, for appraising the value claims of others, there is a strong and constantly improving resource available to all of us: experience. And as each of you come to know that you do a better job of making value judgments now than you did at an earlier stage of life, you also know that you are capable of ranking some value judgments as better than others. As I see it, the examination of your life—what Socrates called for—is best served by carrying on that process assiduously and constantly, and gaining as much experience in doing it as life can possibly offer.

To increase our exposure to values and give ourselves greater practice in adjudging various life situations, we can turn to literature, drama, the arts, and the counsels of the sciences of behavior. Most especially, the works that have become known as "great books" are sources for us of long-tested value beliefs, and deserve especial attention in our search. We can also reflect on the meanings and effects of the day's news and of the events in our personal lives. Virtually anything that we find interesting, unless it is a mere palliative, will assist in this purpose.

So let us close this book and proceed to life.

Suggestions for Further Reading

So far as I know, no works exist, other than this one, that are intended for the general reader on the question "What Is Value?" However, for interested readers I offer the following annotated bibliography to philosophic writings on this and related matters that may be not too abstruse in their language.

Aschenbrenner, Karl. *The Concepts of Value.* Dordrecht: D. Reidel, 1971. A copious collection and examination of words and phrases through which authors and speakers convey valuations.

Dewey, John. *Theory of Valuation.* In *International Encyclopedia of Unified Science,* vol. 2. Chicago: University of Chicago Press, 1939. Dewey regards value as a quality of things, whose presence is testable by scientific means. With respect to comparing the present situation with an envisioned better one, Dewey's theory shares a similarity with the present work.

Frankena, William K. "Value and Valuation." In *The Encyclopedia of Philosophy*, ed. Paul Edwards. New York: Macmillan, 1967. A brief and most useful historic and thematic survey of the problem of value.

Goldthwait, John T. *Value, Language, and Life.* Amherst, N.Y.: Prometheus Books, 1985. This is my own work setting forth in full philosophical argument the value theory, which I call the framing-concept theory of value, on which this present book is based.

Hall, Everett W. *What Is Value?* New York: The Humanities Press, 1952. Hall works within the very minimal metaphysical presupposition of the analytical philosophy movement, namely, that all that an object of awareness can be is either a property or a relation. He decides that value is neither a property nor a relation, but he does not generate a theory to explain what value is.

Hare, R. M. *The Language of Morals.* New York: Oxford University Press, 1964. Hare is among the first in modern philosophy to work out the special logic of ethical propositions. He gives special study to "value words." Value judgments, as he sees them, all prescribe something to do, an action binding on all persons. He terms his doctrine "prescriptivism."

Moore, G. E. *Principia Ethica.* Cambridge: Cambridge University Press, 1903. Moore avers that the quality of goodness is simple and unanalyzable, and is known by intuition. His is one of several forms of "intuitionism."

Stevenson, Charles L. *Ethics and Language.* New Haven: Yale University Press, 1944. A chief work in the school called "emotivism," basing value on emotion. "This is good," Stevenson says, means a factual report on an emotion, "I approve of this," plus a command, "[You] do so as well."

Index